Comments on other *Amazing Stories* from readers & reviewers

"*Tightly written volumes filled with lots of wit and humour about famous and infamous Canadians.*"
Eric Shackleton, *The Globe and Mail*

"*The heightened sense of drama and intrigue, combined with a good dose of human interest is what sets* Amazing Stories *apart.*"
Pamela Klaffke, *Calgary Herald*

"*This is popular history as it should be... For this price, buy two and give one to a friend.*"
Terry Cook, a reader from Ottawa, on **Rebel Women**

"*Glasner creates the moment of the explosion itself in graphic detail...she builds detail upon gruesome detail to create a convincingly authentic picture.*"
Peggy McKinnon, *The Sunday Herald,* on **The Halifax Explosion**

"*It was wonderful...I found I could not put it down. I was sorry when it was completed.*"
Dorothy F. from Manitoba on **Marie-Anne Lagimodière**

"*Stories are rich in description, and bristle with a clever, stylish realness.*"
Mark Weber, *Central Alberta Advisor,* on **Ghost Town Stories II**

"*A compelling read. Bertin...has selected only the most intriguing tales, which she narrates with a wealth of detail.*"
Joyce Glasner, *New Brunswick Reader,* on **Strange Events**

"*The resulting book is one readers will want to share with all the women in their lives.*"
Lynn Martel, *Rocky Mountain Outlook,* on **Women Explorers**

GREAT LEFT WINGERS

GREAT LEFT WINGERS

Stars of Hockey's Golden Age

HOCKEY

by Chris Robinson

PUBLISHED BY ALTITUDE PUBLISHING CANADA LTD.
1500 Railway Avenue, Canmore, Alberta T1W 1P6
www.altitudepublishing.com
www.amazingstories.ca
1-800-957-6888

Extreme care has been taken to ensure that all information presented in
this book is accurate and up to date. Neither the author nor the
publisher can be held responsible for any errors.

Publisher	Stephen Hutchings
Associate Publisher	Kara Turner
Series Editor	Jim Barber
Editors	Linda Aspen-Baxter and Nancy MacKenzie
Cover and layout	Bryan Pezzi

We acknowledge the financial support of the Government
of Canada through the Book Publishing Industry Development
Program (BPIDP) for our publishing activities.

Altitude GreenTree Program
Altitude Publishing will plant twice as many trees as were used
in the manufacturing of this product.

Library and Archives Canada Cataloguing in Publication

Robinson, Chris, 1967-
   Great left wingers / Chris Robinson.

(Amazing stories)
Includes bibliographical references.
ISBN 1-55439-082-6

   1. Hockey players--Biography. 2. National Hockey League--Biography.
3. Hockey--Offense. I. Title. II. Series: Amazing stories (Canmore, Alta.)

GV848.5.A1R62 2006   796.962'092'2   C2005-906890-6

Printed and bound in Canada by Friesens
2 4 6 8 9 7 5 3 1

For Busher and Scarface

Contents

Prologue

The Detroit Red Wings opened the first round of the 1956 Stanley Cup playoffs against the Toronto Maple Leafs. Detroit won the first two games at home. Game two was a tight-checking, violent affair. Elbows, sticks, fists, and bodychecks were delivered with reckless abandon.

As usual, Detroit's left winger, Ted Lindsay, was in the middle of things. In the second period, Lindsay and Toronto's Tod Sloan engaged in a nasty stick swinging incident that left Lindsay with a bloody gash above his eye. Later in the game, Gordie Howe hammered Sloan into the boards. Sloan had to be carried off because he had suffered a broken shoulder. His season was finished.

With the Leafs down 2–0, the series headed back to Toronto, where Leafs fans were in a grim mood. The day of game three, a man called Toronto newspapers and warned, "Don't worry about Howe and Lindsay tonight. I'm going to shoot them if they play in the game."

At first, Lindsay and Howe knew nothing of the threat because they had been staying at a hotel in Hamilton. However, in Toronto, the story was big news. "Will Shoot Howe, Lindsay, To Avenge Sloan, is Threat," said one headline.

Lindsay and Howe did not hear about the threat until

they arrived at Maple Leaf Gardens for the game. On the surface, neither man took the call too seriously. Their Detroit teammates even tried to make light of the situation. Red Wing defenceman, Bob Goldham, jokingly suggested that rookie Cummy Burton skate out for the warm-up with Howe's number nine on his back and Lindsay's number seven on the front. Burton was then supposed to skate up and down the ice to see what happened. Burton refused, of course.

Beneath the laughs, though, there was genuine concern. Undercover policemen were on the watch throughout the Gardens. The threat clearly rattled the Wings. Just 29 seconds into the game, Toronto's George Armstrong scored to give the Leafs an early lead. Throughout the first two periods, the Wings looked nervous and hesitant. With just over 10 minutes remaining in the game, they found themselves down 4–2. Gordie Howe scored on a sizzling 36-foot slapshot to bring the Wings to within one point of a tie. Then it was Lindsay's turn.

With five minutes remaining and the Wings down 4–3, Lindsay decided that he'd had enough. He was going to show Toronto just what he thought of their threats....

Chapter 1
Aurel Joliat

When a slight man of almost 80 years stepped out onto the ice during an old-timers' game at the Ottawa Civic Centre in 1981, young hockey fans might have had no idea that this fragile man with the black cap was a Montreal Canadiens' legend. Aurel Joliat was the first of the Flying Frenchmen. As this tiny, thin man stepped on the ice, time reversed. He became a little giant. As soon as his feet touched the ice, a boyish glow beamed from beneath his cap. His skating was smooth and confident. Civic Centre fans roared their approval.

Legend has it that Montrealers should count their blessings that Aurel Joliat ever played a shift with the Montreal Canadiens. On his way from Ottawa to Regina to find work as a harvester, Joliat briefly joined the Iroquois Falls Flyers of the

Northern Ontario Hockey League. Prior to a championship game, Joliat was approached by "a couple of smooth gents with beady eyes" who offered him $500 to throw the game. Joliat had never seen that much money in his life. He quickly grabbed the money and promised a fortune for all. The sinister duo went off and placed as many bets as they could on the opposing team. Meanwhile, Joliat showed up for the game with a train ticket in his travel bag.

The Flyers won the game with ease. After the game, the two men rushed to the Flyers' dressing room to find Joliat. While they were outside, Joliat went out a back exit, headed to the railroad station, and hopped aboard a train to Regina. On the train, Joliat sat back and counted his cash. Then he smiled and thought of the six goals he had scored that night for the Flyers.

Joliat never returned to Iroquois Falls. However, it was that kind of fast manoeuvring that made Aurel Joliat a superstar in the NHL for 16 years and one of greatest left wingers of his time. Joliat was five foot six inches and 135 pounds. That made him one of the smallest and lightest players in NHL history, but he was one of the fastest, slickest, and toughest players of his era. For 16 years, Aurel Joliat and his famous black cap starred with the Montreal Canadiens playing alongside the great Howie Morenz. The Canadiens' roster also included future Hall of Famers Sprague Cleghorn, Georges Vezina, Joe Malone, and Sylvio Mantha. Led by Joliat and Morenz, the Canadiens became known as the Flying Frenchmen.

"The Mighty Atom" or "The Little Giant," as Joliat was called because of his small size but incredible skill, helped lead the Canadiens to their first three NHL-era Stanley Cups. He also won the Hart Trophy in 1934 and was an all-star four times. As Morenz once said of his friend and linemate: "If it wasn't for Joliat, you wouldn't be writing about me so much."

Aurel Joliat was born in Ottawa in 1901 to a Swiss immigrant and learned to skate on the Rideau Canal with boyhood chums and future NHLers Bill and Frank Boucher. Joliat excelled in hockey and football in the Ottawa area. He should have been a football star. He started as a punter and fullback with the Ottawa Rough Riders and at season's end headed to Regina to do some harvesting.

"There were harvest excursion trains in those days for guys who wanted to go out West and do harvesting. I met two fellows who knew my brother and they said, 'We're going to a football practice and you're coming with us. We need players.'"

Joliat agreed and joined the Regina Boat Club football team. Joliat's stay was brief.

"On my third or fourth game against Moose Jaw, I break my leg in three places."

That was the end of Joliat's football career. While Joliat was laid-up, he received a visit that changed the course of his life.

"I'm stuck in my hotel with crutches," remembered Joliat, "Just before Christmas 1920, about 11 o'clock at night,

I come face-to-face with a man who said, 'You're Joliat, aren't you? Well, my name is Pindar and I own the Saskatoon club of the Prairies Professional Hockey League. I want you to play for me."

Joliat showed the man his crutches and said he couldn't play.

"That's all right," said Pindar. "You'll heal and we need players. Come to Saskatoon, now."

Joliat agreed but said he had no train fare.

"That's all right," said Pindar. "Jump on the first train and just tell them Bob Pindar said it would be okay for you to travel."

"And would you believe it worked?" said Joliat. "I stayed at a hotel he owned, and everything was paid. After a while, I'd go to practice with the team, playing defence of all things. Well, on the third morning, Rusty Crawford, who used to play for the old Quebec Bulldogs, lets go a hard shot that hits my right leg. That was it."

By that time, Joliat was in enormous pain and homesick. Pindar gave Joliat $100 and said, "Don't forget you are a pro now, and I want you to come back to play for me next year."

"Five minutes later," said Joliat, "I was on a train for Ottawa. I practised for the Saskatoon Sheiks the next winter, but my leg was still bad and I never got to play for Pindar in 1921–1922 season."

Joliat was all set to join the Sheiks for the 1922–1923 season.

"I was supposed to play for Pindar in 1922–1923. But that year, Leo Dandurand, who owned the Canadiens, also wanted me to play for him because he had been told that I was pretty good. He came right here to the Chateau Laurier in Ottawa to try and convince me to sign."

Joliat refused and said he was obligated to Pindar. The next morning, Joliat opened the daily newspaper to read that he'd been traded by Saskatoon to the Montreal Canadiens for their veteran superstar, Newsy Lalonde. It was one of the most controversial trades of the time. The hockey world was stunned. The Canadiens had given up an aging star for an unknown amateur. Montreal fans were outraged by the deal. Dandurand instantly became the most unpopular person in Montreal. Faced with a barrage of hateful phone calls about the trade, Dandurand even had to have his phone disconnected.

"Lalonde was about 40 years old at the time," remembered Joliat, "And he had become a problem. He and [teammate] Sprague Cleghorn used to fight during practices. There was a lot of animosity among the players, and Danduran thought that getting rid of Lalonde would solve things."

Lalonde wasn't bothered by the trade because Dandurand had negotiated a new contract for him that ensured he received twice what he had been getting paid as a Canadien. However, he didn't like the idea of a kid coming in and taking his job. When Montreal played Saskatoon in an exhibition game during Joliat's second year with the

Canadiens, Lalonde let "The Mighty Atom" know what he thought of being replaced.

"In the second period, after two or three rushes from my left wing, I started another one," said Joliat in 1984. "Well, he [Lalonde] was the big rooster at everything he played in those days, and I was the 21 year old kid who had taken his place with the Canadiens. He was waiting for me. One second I was on left wing; the next I was on right wing. He crushed me, split my mouth in two. The dirty son of a...."

Joliat made his debut with the Canadiens in October 1922. When the petite forward stepped onto the ice for the first time, the fans booed. When Joliat scored two goals in his first game, the stunned hecklers fell silent. He finished his rookie season third in team scoring and helped lead the Canadiens into the playoffs for the first time in four years. It was an astonishing debut. Joliat was one of the few players to successfully make the jump from amateur to professional. Montreal fans quickly forgot all about Newsy Lalonde.

Joliat joined a team and league that was struggling to survive. The NHL had only four teams: the Hamilton Tigers, Toronto St. Pats, Ottawa Senators, and Montreal Canadiens. The league was financially unstable and desperately hoping to add teams from the United States. More teams would expand their fan base and bring in new revenues. To do that, they needed star players who could electrify the crowds and use speed and power to capture the imaginations of American fans who weren't familiar with the game.

Dandurand felt that the Montreal Canadiens were just the team to ignite the crowd.

When Dandurand purchased the team in 1921, he said, "Hockey always has been a game of weight and power, and a small man needed a great deal of skill to make it as a pro. I believe that speed and skill are the best ingredients of the game. I view the Canadiens as playing a very fast, slick game but not being bullied by anyone."

Under Dandurand's savvy guidance, the team slowly built a nucleus of exciting young players to capture the hearts and souls of hockey fans across the continent. One of those players was Aurel Joliat. The following season, Montreal signed a young centre named Howie Morenz. The speedy and gifted Morenz was placed on a line with Joliat. The two clicked immediately, and together, Joliat and Morenz helped make Dandurand's vision come true.

In the playoffs, Morenz, Joliat, and Bill Boucher, Joliat's childhood buddy from Ottawa, led the Canadiens to an upset victory of the Ottawa Senators before sweeping the Vancouver Maroons and Calgary Tigers in the Stanley Cup finals.

Joliat fondly remembered a goal he scored in the play-offs against Calgary. "I travelled through the entire Calgary team and faked a shot to the far corner of the net. But even as I let go, I sensed I was covered on the play. So I kept going, rounded the net, and backhanded a shot into the open corner. I tumbled head over heels after that one. We went on to the win the Cup, and I consider it the best goal I ever scored."

In their first year together, Joliat and Morenz led Montreal to their first NHL-era Stanley Cup victory. The following season, Joliat and Morenz got even better. The two combined for 56 goals, and Joliat led the league with a career-best 29 goals. The Canadiens returned to the Stanley Cup finals, but lost to Victoria. Over the next 11 years, Morenz and Joliat led the Canadiens to two more Stanley Cup championships and became hockey's most fearsome duo.

Thanks in large part to the excitement generated by Morenz and Joliat, hockey's equivalent of baseball superstars Babe Ruth and Lou Gehrig, the NHL was a 10-team league by 1927. Six of those franchises were from the United States. Morenz, Joliat, and the rest of the "Flying Frenchmen" brought fans out of their seats.

"When the Canadiens and Howie Morenz came to town," said Dandurand, no stranger to hyperbole, "the American teams beat their drums hard about the games. That attracted the casual fan who went to see hockey out of curiosity. But they only had to watch the Canadiens' approach to the game and they were hooked."

The Flying Frenchmen earned their nickname due to the team's blazing speed and French roots; ironically, neither Morenz nor Joliat could speak the language.

"Morenz may have been 'the Babe Ruth of Hockey,'" remembered former Canadien Johnny Gagnon, Joliet and Morenz's linemate throughout most of the 30s, "but Joliat was more of an artist, a stickhandler. Aurel always made beautiful passes. He wasn't as fast as Morenz, but he could move when he wanted to. Joliat skated with short, choppy strides and manipulated the puck as if it were stuck to his stick."

Gagnon, a speedy right winger who was nicknamed the "Black Cat," joined the Canadiens in 1929–1930. Initially, he had problems adjusting to his new linemates.

"At first, I had a little trouble playing with Howie. He wasn't too good as a playmaker so I'd play more with Aurel. He always used to get the puck and pass it to me, and then I'd pass it to him. We had pretty much the same stickhandling style, and I always knew the kind of moves he'd make. For instance, as soon as he hit the blue line, he'd throw me a pass behind his back."

As Jim Coleman of *The Globe and Mail* once wrote: "He [Joliat] would dodge, flit, and with split-second timing, he could back pedal, evading the most formidable body checks, leaving some large and embarrassed defensemen floundering on the ice."

During one memorable game in the 1930s, Joliat controlled the puck during a penalty kill for a minute and a half. The Forum fans gave him a standing ovation.

"I remembering killing a couple of two-minute penalties by going up and down the ice with the puck," said Joliat. "Those guys were chasing me crazy."

Joliat might not have had Morenz's speed, but according to Ranger Frank Boucher, he was "as slippery as Howie Morenz was swift." Joliat's quickness was so frustrating that

Aurel Joliat

during one game, Babe Dye of the Toronto Maple Leafs skated over to the Montreal bench and said to Canadiens owner, Leo Dandurand, "I'm tired of chasing that shadow of yours, the Flying Frenchman Joliat. Move him to centre, hold a mirror to each side of him, and you'll have the fastest line in hockey."

"One shift my first year, I remember I tried to run him through the boards," said former Boston Bruin Bill Cowley, in 1986. "He put a deke on me, and I almost went through the boards myself. I was trying to knock that black cap off his head, and he skated by me and said, 'Don't try that again, young fella.' He was small but nobody could hit him. If they did, he could handle himself."

When opponents did get Joliat, he unleashed a vicious temper and shied away from no one.

"He was smaller, you understand," wrote Jim Coleman, "and he fought back in his own way. He was singularly adept at sinking the butt end of his stick into the opponent's ribs."

There was one act in particular that drove Joliat into an instant rage. He loved to wear his little black cap and was perhaps a tad sensitive about his increasingly balding head.

"I used to wear them," said Joliat, "because it was cold in the rinks in those days. But the peaks were too big … like a baseball cap. So, I trimmed them down, and got them good and tight, so they couldn't knock it off."

Players loved to goad him about the cap and sometimes even tried to knock it off. When that happened, Joliat went ballistic, and if the offender escaped unscathed, he was fortunate.

A fallen cap wasn't the only thing that could incense Joliat. During a 1925 game against the Canadiens' archrivals, the Montreal Maroons, Joliat flew into a fury when a goal he thought he'd scored was disallowed. He raced towards the goal judge and started to swing his stick at him. The judge, a former hockey player named Ernie Russell, reacted quickly.

He grabbed Joliat's stick before he could do any harm. The incident should have ended there, except that a number of Canadiens' fans had stormed into the goal judge's cage and pinned Russell to the wall. Joliat's linemate, Billy Boucher, skated in and bashed Russell with his stick.

Incredibly, while all this was taking place, the game was still continuing. Nels Stewart of the Maroons skated up the ice and scored. The referees, who apparently hadn't noticed the small riot going on in the goal judge's cage, signalled a goal for the Maroons. Canadiens' fans were furious. Meanwhile, the Maroons fans were incensed that neither Boucher nor Joliat had been penalized. Fights broke out in the stands. Fortunately, police restored order before things got completely out of control. The Canadiens ended up winning the game 7–4.

"I lost most of the fights, of course," said Joliat. "But, I won one in Montreal. It was against the chief of police. He was at the game as a spectator. He jumped on the ice during a brawl against the Maroons, and I belted him. He was wearing a big, racoon hat. I pulled it off him. I got the better of that one, all right."

Joliat also had a sense of humour. He rarely showed his emotions on the ice, but during a game against the Montreal Maroons, Joliat was hammered into the boards by the Maroon's Red Dutton. Both men fell. Joliat's cap and stick slid across the ice. Joliat was furious when he got to his feet. He grabbed his hat and smashed it back on his head. To add insult to injury, Dutton picked up Joliat's stick and handed it to him, grinning. Joliat snatched the stick and turned in anger. Then, for a moment, his face broke into a smile at Dutton's comic gesture.

Like Maurice Richard, who followed them, Morenz and Joliat had a flare for the dramatic. It was the final game of the 1931 Stanley Cup finals. Two of the first four games had been decided in overtime. With the series tied at two wins apiece, the Black Hawks came out flying against the weary Canadiens. Only Joliat's ferocious checking and stopping five rushes kept the Black Hawks from scoring. The game remained scoreless until Joliat and Morenz worked their magic.

"Morenz had rushed away from us with the puck down centre ice and was checked at the defence," remembered Joliat in 1961. "Some Chicago forward picked it up on the gallop, and I checked him at centre. I had taken only two strides when I heard 'Joliat!' screamed at me from the right wing. It was Morenz who had raced back on my left wing, whirled around behind me, and was now under full steam down right. I gave him a pass. He took it at full speed and went clean through the defence to beat goalie, Charlie Gardner. Even Rocket Richard could never make me forget that moment."

The Canadiens scored one more to earn a 2–0 win and their second straight Stanley Cup.

On February 8, 1934, a standing room only crowd braved the bitter cold to honor Aurel Joliat as one of hockey's greatest left wingers. "The Little Giant" was playing in his 500th game. The Canadiens were playing their archenemy, the Montreal Maroons. Joliat stood at centre ice, surrounded by his Montreal Canadiens teammates. Following a thunderous ovation, speeches were delivered and gifts were presented. The evening was so sentimental that even Maroon's Captain Hooley Smith, who was easily Joliat's single worst enemy on the ice that night, skated over and congratulated him.

Then the puck was dropped. The Maroons took full advantage of the ceremony to score two fast goals on the listless Canadiens. Suddenly, Joliat came streaking down the left wing. Using his dazzling stickhandling, Joliat eluded one Maroon after another. As he approached the Maroons' goal, he snapped the puck into the net.

In the third period, Joliat led a rush into the Maroons' zone. He drew the goaltender out and then fed a pass to teammate, Pit Lepine, who fired the puck into the open net. The Forum fans exploded. Thanks to Joliat's heroics, the Canadiens were back in the game.

As the game shifted into high gear, the good will of the pre-game ceremonies faded fast. Fists flew as fights erupted all over the ice. Referee Mike Rodden was kicked in the head by a skate while trying to separate two players.

At the end of regulation time, the score was tied 2–2. The Maroons spoiled the evening by winning 3–2 in overtime. The Canadiens may have lost, but Joliat's play was typical of his entire career. As he so often proved, size was no measure of a man's heart and determination. Joliat's inspired play almost single-handedly lifted his team back into the game.

That season would turn out to be one of Joliat's most memorable. A few months later, the NHL awarded the 35 year old Joliat with the Hart Trophy as the league's most valuable player.

With the peaks, though, came the valleys. While Joliat seemed to get better with age, Morenz was slowing down.

"He just ran out of gas completely when he was about 32 or 33, and that was it," said Joliat. "It nearly broke his heart."

After an injury-riddled, eight-goal season in 1933–1934, the Canadiens traded Morenz to Chicago. Joliat and Gagnon suffered without their linemate, as did the entire team. Within a year, the Canadiens had slipped to the bottom of the standings.

Prior to the 1936–1937 season, the Canadiens surprised everyone when they acquired Morenz from the New York Rangers. Morenz seemed rejuvenated by the return to Montreal. He'd lost some of his power and speed, but the reunited trio of Morenz, Joliat, and Gagnon provided Montreal fans with a few thrills and led the team to first place in the season standings early in the season.

Then tragedy struck. During a game against Chicago in January 1937, Howie Morenz circled around behind the Chicago net. He caught his skate in the boards. As Black Hawks' defenceman Earl Siebert checked Morenz, he stumbled on top of the Canadiens' superstar. With his skate still trapped in the boards, Morenz's leg snapped. His leg was broken, and his career was finished.

"I cried that night," said Joliat. "I knew he wouldn't be back. We were very close, and I knew that Howie was worried about the fact that he might burn himself out early. When his leg shattered that night, I knew there was no way he could come back. He was through, and we all knew it."

Less than two months later, while still in hospital, Morenz died of a heart attack.

Joliat visited his friend and linemate on many occasions at the hospital and remembered what turned out to be his final visit. "Howie suddenly decided to show me he could walk across the room on his crutches. I saw him totter as he started back. I grabbed him and helped him back to bed. He kind of smiled at me and told me, 'I'll be up there watching you in the playoffs.' That was the last thing he said to me."

Joliat's career died with Morenz. By 1945 Joliat was the oldest player in the NHL, and the six shoulder separations, three broken ribs, five nose fractures, and all his other injuries were taking their toll. He played one more year after Morenz's death, but the flare and passion were gone. He scored only 13 points and retired after the season.

Joliat was inducted into the Hockey Hall of Fame in 1945, and two years later, the Canadiens held an Aurel Joliat night at the Montreal Forum. As he stood at centre ice in civilian clothes and his little black cap, a thunderous ovation welcomed him. Joliat received a scroll representing his entry into the Hall of Fame and a cheque for almost $10,000.

Joliat, like all the players of his era, could not live off his hockey savings. By that time, he was working for the Canadian National Railway. He called the financial gesture one of the great thrills of his life.

"It's too much," an emotional Joliat said later. "Too much for a guy like me."

Even in his 60s, Joliat remained feisty and competitive. Prior to a Hockey Hall of Fame dinner in Boston in 1960, Joliat and former Ottawa Senator Punch Broadbent got into an argument over an incident that had taken place in a game 50 years earlier. Later, during dinner, the two men started shouting at each other, and finally, Joliat leaped over the table and started fighting Broadbent.

"The two of them really went at it," recalled Ottawa hockey historian Bill Galloway.

By the time the two were finally pulled apart, the two men were cut and bleeding. Finally, NHL commissioner Clarence Campbell intervened and convinced the men to take a breath and return to their rooms. During the group photo session after the dinner, Joliat and Broadbent were missing. Their faces were such a mess that Clarence Campbell refused to allow them in the picture.

When asked about the fight, Joliat said, "Broadbent didn't beat me in 1924, and he sure as hell isn't going to do it in 1960."

Joliat was on the ice again in Ottawa in January 1985, this time as part of a tribute to Montreal's all-time greats. Beliveau, Richard, Harvey, Plante, and Dickie Moore were all there. With so many stars in attendance, it would have taken someone special to steal the show — someone like Aurel Joliat. The Forum crowd roared as Joliat, wearing a Canadiens' uniform and his famous black cap, leaped onto the ice and skated around the face-off circle. As the ovation continued to grow, Joliat lost his balance and fell.

"It seemed as if the voice of the crowd had knocked him over," wrote David Gowdey in his story, *The Return of Aurel Joliat.*

After refusing various attempts to assist him, Joliat helped himself up. The roar grew louder. Joliat grabbed the puck at centre ice and started towards the net where the great Habs' goalie, Gump Worsley, was waiting. He skated too close to the red carpet and did a somersault on the ice. No one helped him that time.

Joliat grimaced and then smiled. As he got to his feet, he straightened his cap, picked up the puck, and headed towards the net. As he skated across the goal-mouth and swept the puck past Worsley, the Forum crowd roared their approval. Joliat took off his cap and waved to the Forum faithful.

Joliat skated back to centre, and Doug Harvey and Toe Blake lifted him by the arms onto the red carpet. Joliat briefly stood at centre ice one last time. As the applause rained down, Joliat must have been reminded of a time 60 years earlier when in the same Montreal Forum, he and Howie Morenz captured the hearts and souls of hockey fans everywhere.

Joliat died in 1986, three months short of his 85th birthday. He lived his life with the same passion and fire that made him one of hockey's greatest.

In a passage that could easily serve as Joliat's epitaph, a writer from Joliat's era wrote: "He rolled away from 200-pounders, faded from the path of charging rivals, and side-stepped and hurdled his way clear of smashing body-blows, flying elbows and jabbing butt-ends. His amazing quickness saved him from untold punishment over the years and kept him going, like a brook, apparently forever."

Chapter 2
Harvey "Busher" Jackson

During the depression years, when many were struggling just to find food and work, Toronto Maple Leafs' left winger, Harvey "Busher" Jackson, had it all. On the ice as part of the famous Kid Line with Charlie Conacher and Joe Primeau, Jackson dazzled opponents with his speed and skills. Off the ice, Jackson's shining smile, movie star looks, spendthrift ways, and swanky cars made him the nearest thing to a swinging superstar that hockey had until Bobby Hull came along. Girls, boys, men, and women all adored Jackson.

"Those were the days," wrote *The Globe and Mail*'s Scott Young, "when the sight of Busher taking one of Primeau's passes and cutting in on goal made the hackles rise on all who saw it.... Those were the days when Busher and some of the others would head out after a game and pile into their roadsters and go to dance most of the night at the Silver Slipper."

Hardly a week passed without seeing details of Jackson's exploits in the headlines: BUSHER SCORES THREE IN TORONTO VICTORY. BUSHER SHINES AS LEAFS WIN OVER RANGERS. BUSHER GETS GAME'S ONLY GOAL IN OVER-TIME. BUSHER THE GREATEST, LESTER PATRICK SAYS. TWO CLEVER GOALS BY JACKSON THRILL LARGE CROWD.

"The Busher," Leafs owner Conn Smythe once said, "had the world by the tail."

It wouldn't last. It couldn't last, but Busher didn't want to believe that. He thought the good times would be as certain as the sun, that the adoration, parties, and the cash would flow each new day. He had come a long way from where he first learned to play hockey on a rink in west end Toronto called "Poverty Pond."

"When I first started to play," remembered Jackson in a 1966 *Globe Magazine* article, "there was a rink we used to call Poverty Pond. I never had any skates, so I borrowed a pair — I stole a pair, to be exact, but whose did they happen to be? My cousin's, a girl, so I was skating on girl's skates the first time I ever skated."

Jackson earned spending money in those days by shoveling ice, delivering newspapers, and cashing in empty pop bottles, but at heart, he was a rink rat. He spent every free moment on the ice.

"You had to make your own breaks then. But I loved the game and I'd go miles to play — I used to play on Saturday afternoons when most of the kids would go to a show or something. You've got to love the game to play it that way."

Another place Jackson played was on Grenadier Pond in Toronto. It was there that he learned how to take passes. "You learned how to take a pass there, because if you missed it, you might have to skate about a mile before you ever saw the puck again."

At age 15, Jackson had his first hockey job — working for a broker on Bay Street so that he could play for their hockey team, the Brokers. That same year, Toronto's old stockyard club, T&Y Mercantile League, drafted Jackson to help an injury-depleted team out for a game. Jackson immediately impressed player-coach Bert Hodges and ended up staying in the league. When it came time to discuss a contract, Jackson simply asked "for enough money to buy a shirt and shoes, to make up for the money he'd lose by not scraping the ice."

Jackson quit high school and began working for the club. In March 1928, Jackson led the Stockyards team to the championship of the Big Six Mercantile League. With the championship game in overtime, Jackson scored on a fluke play. He lifted the puck into the air, and few, if any, players on the ice seemed to know where it had gone. A moment later, it sank into the Goodyear net. The goalie had not even seen the puck drop out of the air.

Jackson played within the old stockbrokers' league for a year before it went bankrupt. Fortunately, by that time, Jackson had other alternatives.

Jackson's hockey career really began at the Ravina Garden's indoor rink. Jackson decided that he wanted to play there because that's where the big boys played. He went to the rink one day, but found the doors locked. After several knocks, an attendant finally answered, took a quick look at Jackson, and chased him away. Unfazed, Jackson came back to the rink so often that the rink manager finally invited the boy in and made him an offer. Jackson could come in, put on his skates, then grab a shovel, and start clearing the ice. Jackson wouldn't be paid, but he would be allowed to do some skating and puck-handling.

One day, as Jackson was skating, Frank Selke and his Junior A team, the Toronto Marlboros, came onto the ice. The Marlies were a good team, but this brash young kid began skating through and around them. No one could get the puck from Jackson. Selke asked an assistant who the kid was, but he didn't know and suggested that they throw him off the ice. Instead, Selke called Jackson over and asked him if he was a signed player.

"Haven't signed and don't want to sign," said the cocky Jackson.

"All right then," replied Selke, "you'll have to get off the ice."

"Let me play and I'll sign after practice," said Jackson.

"No!" said Selke, "Here's a form. Sign on this line or take your skates off."

The stubborn Jackson knew a good opportunity when he saw it. He kept his skates on and signed the contract.

Playing on a line with Eddie Convey and future Maple Leaf linemate Charlie Conacher, Jackson excelled with the Marlboros. He scored four goals in the four regular season games he played. Then he exploded in the playoffs, scoring an incredible 16 points in three games. The following season, 1928–1929, Jackson's line continued their torrid pace. During the Marlboro's successful Memorial Cup run, Jackson led the team with an astonishing 40 points in 13 games.

By that time, Jackson's hockey exploits were well known around Toronto. In describing a 1929 game, the *Toronto Star* wrote: "Of course no one will take the star position away from Harvey Jackson. Jackson did not get on the score sheet, but he stood out in a collection of real classy junior players. Every time he grabbed the disc, the students ganged him four deep. He made a lot of spectacular plays and got away a score of hard shots, but he was back-checked and pestered so much that he seldom got a real chance to score himself. But he wasn't selfish with the puck and fed his comrades nicely. Jackson is probably the best junior in the game today."

In 1926, Conn Smythe was hired to put together players for the New York Rangers, a new NHL franchise. Despite assembling a first-rate roster, Smythe was fired because Rangers' owner, John Hammond, felt that Smythe hadn't

acquired enough recognizable talent. As part of his settle-
ment, the Rangers gave Smythe cash and the rights to Joe
Primeau. An angry Smythe promptly used the money to buy
the NHL's mediocre Toronto St. Pats. Smythe immediately
changed the name of the team to the Maple Leafs.

Heading into their third season in 1929–1930, the Maple
Leafs remained a mediocre team. To help out veterans
Ace Bailey and Harold "Baldy" Cotton, Smythe added the
smooth-skating playmaker named Joe Primeau, and then he
signed Charlie Conacher from the Marlboros. Jackson was
livid that he wasn't signed as well. Jackson refused to sign
with the Marlboros, and a rumour spread that Jackson had
told Leafs' owner Conn Smythe that he would instantly turn
the team around if they signed him.

On December 6, 1929, Jackson got his wish. The following night, at 18 years of age, he became the youngest player in
the NHL. During his debut against the Montreal Canadiens,
Jackson announced his arrival by flattening Canadiens' legend Howie Morenz.

While on the ice, Morenz looked up at Jackson and said,
"You'll do."

With the Leafs losing the game, Smythe tinkered with
his lines. Late in the third period, he put Jackson on a line
with Conacher and Primeau. The line didn't score that night,
but they had a number of excellent scoring chances. The
Kid Line was born, at least momentarily. However, it would
be weeks before the trio played together again. During his

debut, Jackson suffered a charley horse, and then Conacher was out with tonsillitis.

It was while he was injured that Jackson got his famous nickname. Prior to a game against the New York Americans, Leafs' trainer Tim Daly asked Jackson to help him carry the hockey sticks.

"I'm not here to carry sticks. I'm here to play hockey," answered Jackson smugly.

"You ain't nothing but a fresh busher!" Daly retorted.

At the time, a "busher" meant a player who was impetuous and arrogant. The nickname "Busher" stuck.

Jackson was so self-assured that prior to a game against Chicago, legend has it that Leafs' goalie, Lorne Chabot, gave Jackson a tap with his stick and wished him "Good luck."

The brash Jackson replied, "Don't you worry about me, Chabot. You just keep 'em out. I'll put 'em in."

True to his word, Jackson delivered. He was something special. He could score with the best of them, but the beauty of Busher Jackson was the way he "put 'em in." He moved down the wing with the grace of a dancer, the speed of the wind, and the strength of the gods. He was one of the greatest rushers of his or any other era because he possessed those talents — plus he had something unusual: a natural shift.

"He comes at you," said Red Dutton, a former defencemen with the New York Americans, "taking a stroke on his left skate, and then instead of taking the next stroke with his right foot, he seems to take another with his left."

Jackson could cut left or right with an almost perfect fake. He often weaved past a defenceman so closely that they brushed sweaters.

"Now, Jackson was a beautiful skater," recalled Tom Gaston in *A Fan for All Seasons,* "just like a hula dancer on skates. He had this great maneuverability; he could just go through that defence like nobody's business. He wasn't really a tough guy, but he could take care of himself if he had to. And boy, did the girls love him. He looked just like a Hollywood movie star."

"Busher is so fast," recalled Jackson's teammate, Hap Day, in *The Leafs: The First 50 Years,* "that one night in Montreal, he circled the net, started down the ice, and shot the puck when he was nearing centre. And do you know what? He was travelling so fast that he caught up with the puck and passed it before he got to the blue line."

The era of the Kid Line began officially in late December 1929. With the team playing poorly, Smythe moved Joe Primeau onto a line with Charlie Conacher and Harold "Baldy" Cotton. When Cotton got injured, Jackson took his place. In their first game, Primeau set up Conacher and Jackson for goals.

The next day, Lou Marsh of the *Toronto Star* wrote: "The kid line showed well." The Kid Line was born.

"We had our little playmaker there, Joe Primeau, who

would give you the puck just where you wanted it," recalled Jackson in the 1950s. "Charlie and I were always wanting it, both of us, all the time. I remember one night in the dressing room, Charlie and I were arguing about which one should have got a pass on one play, and we were going at it so hot and heavy that finally Primeau threw down his stick and gloves and said, 'I'm going to cut the puck in half from now on and give one half to one guy and one to the other.'"

The trio liked to have a little fun, too. During a 1931 Christmas Eve game, they pulled a fast one on Montreal's Howie Morenz. The teams were tied 1–1. Every time Morenz took a face-off, he complained to Primeau that he wanted to be home with his family for Christmas. When the buzzer finally sounded to end the overtime, the teams went to their dressing rooms. However, the referee called them back to the ice after he discovered that there were still 10 seconds remaining.

Morenz was furious. "There's not time for anything to happen! It's a farce!" he screamed at the referee.

Morenz then turned to Primeau and said, "When he drops the puck, let it lie there and we'll use the 10 seconds up that way." Primeau agreed. However, when the puck was dropped, Primeau suddenly tapped the puck towards the left side where Jackson was skating full speed. Jackson took the puck in stride, skated away from his check, used a defence-man for a screen, and scored on an ankle-high shot. Primeau later denied that it was a planned play and that he'd aimlessly tapped the puck, but Morenz was incensed.

"Morenz and I were still parked stock-still at centre ice," recalled Joe Primeau years later. "You should have heard Morenz then. He thought the play had been planned."

Even the addition of the Kid Line couldn't help the Leafs immediately. They finished out of the playoffs in 1929–1930. The following season, bolstered by the addition of rugged defenceman, King Clancy, and the improved play of Conacher, Jackson, and Primeau, the Leafs played well and finished second in the Canadian division. Despite an early round loss to Chicago in the 1930–1931 playoffs, it was clear that the Leafs were starting to gel.

Heading into the 1931–1932 season, Toronto was buzzing about the Maple Leafs. On November 12, 1931, the team debuted in their new state of the art arena, Maple Leaf Gardens. With the new arena and the emergence of the Kid Line, Toronto fans were hopeful that this was the year the Leafs would win their first Stanley Cup championship.

Early on, the team stumbled, prompting Smythe to replace coach Art Duncan with Dick Irvin. Miraculously, Irvin led the Leafs from last place to first in just one month. The Kid Line flourished under Irvin. By season's end, at 21 years of age, Jackson became the youngest player ever to win an NHL scoring championship, finishing with 53 points. Primeau finished second with 50 points, while Conacher led the NHL with 34 goals, making the Kid Line a class of their own.

After beating the Chicago Black Hawks and Montreal

Maroons, the Maple Leafs headed to the Stanley Cup finals for a best of five series against the New York Rangers. Led by Jackson's natural hat trick in game one of the finals and a combined 16 points by the Kid Line in just three games, the Leafs eliminated the Rangers with relative ease. They became the first NHL team to win the Stanley Cup finals in three straight games. After the season, Jackson was named to the first all-star team for the first of four times in his career. During the spring of 1932, the entire country knew of Busher Jackson and the Kid Line.

Jackson was a hero on and off the ice. During the previous summer, Jackson made the headlines when he raced into a blazing cottage on Wasaga Beach and carried two men to safety. In August 1932, Jackson helped organize a search for three youths who had stolen a car and injured a pursuing police officer. "A score of white-flannelled young men, led by Busher Jackson, spent two hours in the bush and swamp searching for the culprits, but without success," said a *Toronto Star* article.

By 1932–1933, Jackson was earning $6,500 a year and spending money like he owned the city. He spent his money freely on fancy cars, girls, clothes, and parties. However, Leafs' owner, Conn Smythe, disapproved of Jackson's carefree lifestyle and reminded him that his hockey career wouldn't last forever. Smythe offered to match any set amount that Jackson put into savings. However, Jackson was his own man and continued to live on the edge.

On the ice, Jackson continued to flourish. On November 20, 1934, Jackson had his most famous night. Heading into the third period, the Leafs were trailing the St. Louis Eagles, formerly the Ottawa Senators, 2–1. In the third period, Toronto came back with four goals; Busher Jackson got all of them.

While the Kid Line continued to put up impressive numbers and terrorize opponents, they never duplicated their fantastic 1931–1932 season. When Joe Primeau retired in 1936, and Charlie Conacher was in and out of the line-up with injuries, the Kid Line was no more. Jackson briefly skated on a line with his younger brother, Art, and late in the 1936–1937 season, Jackson formed another successful line with Gordie Drillon and the great Syl Apps.

Jackson continued to play well, but by 1939, injuries and a troubled personal life began to take their toll.

"Jackson was drinking," recalls Tom Gaston. "Smythe kept it out of the papers back then, but I think he [Jackson] and Conacher were living pretty high. Good-looking boys, huge hockey stars...."

Jackson's goal production decreased from 21 in 1935 to 10 in 1939. Sensing Jackson's career was in a tailspin, Smythe traded him along with teammates Buzz Boll, Doc Romnes, Jimmy Fowler, and Murray Armstrong to the New York Americans on May 18, 1939, in exchange for Hall of Fame left winger, Sweeney Schriner.

While there's no record of Jackson's thoughts on the trade, Smythe only regretted that he hadn't made the trade earlier. "I know now that I should have broken up the Kid Line about 1935 or so. I didn't have the guts. Of course, they were a big gate attraction. I could have found lots of guys to go with Joe Primeau, but he was the only centre who could make Conacher and Jackson click."

It was the end of an era for the Leafs. During Jackson's tenure with Toronto, the team had great success. They won the Canadian division four times and played in six Stanley Cup finals. As good as they were, the Leafs' first Stanley Cup in 1931 was their only championship of the decade.

In his memoirs, Conn Smythe blamed Jackson and Conacher for the Leafs' failure to win more Cups. "Conacher and Jackson never did feel very interested in getting in shape. They were busy driving their new cars and chasing women. Conacher and Jackson were never half as good as they were thought to be. They wanted Joe Primeau to do all the work, and they'd score the goals, which they were pretty good at. But you have to play hockey in three spaces: your end, the middle, and their end. They didn't do it."

After two sub-par seasons with the Americans, Jackson was traded to the Boston Bruins in 1942. Jackson played three seasons for the Bruins; he scored 35 goals and accumulated 78 points in 112 regular season games. He retired after the 1943–1944 campaign.

In 1952, Jackson's name returned to the headlines but for all the wrong reasons. He was charged with assaulting his second wife. During the hearing, Busher's drinking problem became public. Over the next few years, Jackson had more problems at home, and by the end of the 1950s, a series of failed business deals left Jackson in serious debt. Friends tried to help, but Jackson's lax attitude and alcoholism prevented him from keeping jobs.

"I'd rather be the poorest man in the cemetery," Jackson said about his free spending ways. "I helped a lot of people during that time. There wasn't a job around, but somehow people had to eat. I used to like the kids around, too. I'd get them their baseballs and bats and gloves and whatever I could for them."

In another interview, Jackson admitted, "It could be that prosperity came too quickly for me. I was a big leaguer before I realized it. Those were depression years, but I never knew what depression meant — not personally."

Conn Smythe was so disgusted by Jackson's personal life that he prevented Jackson from being inducted into the Hockey Hall of Fame, even when former Kid linemates, Primeau and Conacher, were accepted in 1961.

"I fought for years to keep Busher out of the Hall of Fame," said Smythe in his autobiography. "I'm a hero worshipper myself and he wasn't a good enough person to earn the hero worship of kids."

Primeau and Conacher were outraged, as were fans, players, and media.

"All of us should have made it," said Conacher. "People knew us as a unit."

Smythe argued that Jackson was not eligible because of a Hall of Fame stipulation that said, "Candidates for election shall be chosen on the basis of playing ability, integrity, character, and their contributions to their team." Throughout the 60s, Toronto journalists argued on Jackson's behalf, stating that the requirements were too lofty. They asserted that it was plain hypocritical to allow a noted felon like Black Hawks' owner, Jim Norris, into the Hall of Fame, and not Jackson.

As journalist Dick Beddoes said in March 1966, "I'd say that most people would agree that Jackson should be blackballed from the Temperance Hall of Fame, or even the Chivalry Hall of Fame. But *not* from the Hockey Hall of Fame."

For his part, Jackson just wanted to get into the Hall of Fame before he died so that his son could be with him at the ceremony. He remained bitter about the exclusion.

"They let Babe Ruth into Baseball's Hall of Fame," Jackson once said. "I think he stayed out more nights and got into as much trouble as I did."

It wasn't to be. After being in and out of hospitals throughout the 60s, Jackson returned to hospital on May 2, 1966. This time he didn't leave. Liver disease claimed Jackson's life on June 25, 1966.

In 1971, five years after his death, Busher Jackson was finally admitted to the Hall of Fame. His 16 year old son, Kim, was in attendance at the ceremony and given a guarantee that all of his university costs would be covered. Conn

Smythe was so outraged by the decision that he resigned from the Hall of Fame Induction Committee.

"All I can say," said the belligerent Smythe, "is that the standards are dropping if they let in a man like Jackson."

Jackson never shied away from his difficulties, but when asked if he'd change the way his life had gone, he replied, "I'd do the same thing over again. The first part of my life was pretty exciting. I'll tell you that. It sure gave me pleasure, the game, that is."

"Anyway that's that," wrote *The Telegram*'s Scott Young in 1971. "Busher is in the Hall of Fame. And the record will show that when he took a pass on the fly and cut in off the left wing, the sight of it was like a glimpse of a great work of art. That memory, that true one, now becomes official. The rest is Busher's own business, at long last."

Toronto fans agreed. In 2001, they voted Jackson one of the top 25 Maple Leafs of all-time.

Chapter 3
Doug Bentley

I t was January 21, 1954. The New York Rangers were playing the Boston Bruins. The Rangers trailed Boston by two points for the final playoff spot. There was another reason for the excitement surrounding the game. Two of hockey's greatest duos were reuniting that evening. Thirty-seven year old Doug Bentley hadn't skated with his younger brother, Max, since Max had been traded from the Chicago Black Hawks to the Toronto Maple Leafs seven years earlier. It was Doug's first time on NHL ice in almost two years.

While Max, a notorious hypochondriac, worried about his injuries, many wondered if Doug even had the legs to play after a two-year layoff. It was nothing new for Doug. From the time he showed up at his first NHL training camp, people wondered if the slight, 145-pound left winger had what it took to play with the best players in the world.

When Chicago Black Hawks' president, Bill Tobin, spotted Doug Bentley arriving for their 1939 training camp, he turned to coach Paul Thompson and asked, "Is *he* one of our prospects?"

Thompson nodded his head.

Tobin shook his head and said, "I didn't know things were *that* tough. He's the first walking ghost I've ever seen."

A few days later, Thompson called Tobin. "He's not a walking ghost," said Thompson. "He's a skating ghost. The kid's terrific!"

For the next 12 seasons with the Black Hawks, the 145-pound "ghost," Doug Bentley, was indeed "terrific." Using his tremendous speed and natural goal scoring ability, Bentley scored more than 20 goals in a season six times. He was an all-star three times and won the NHL scoring title once. Bentley also used his blazing speed to help out his defence. He was considered one of the most ferocious back-checkers of his era.

Having already established himself as a regular on the team, Bentley was summoned to the president's office for a raise midway through the 1939–1940 season.

Surprised, Bentley said, "Gee, Mr. Tobin, that's wonderful and I really appreciate it. But if you think I'm good, you should see my brother Max. He's twice as good."

"Is that so?" said the Hawks' president. "Well, in that case, maybe we'd better grab him, too."

Doug and little brother, Max, were just two of 13 Bentley children, of which there were six boys and seven girls. They were born in a town called Delisle, Saskatchewan. Their father, Bill, was among the first immigrants to arrive in the area, in 1903. Bill built a backyard rink and bought skates for all his kids.

"Doug and I used to play road hockey ... just sticks and balls. We'd be three hours every day, chasing the ball around, deking each other, all that stuff. The old rink, where we played on skates, was real narrow and probably helped [our] stickhandling."

The Bentley family was legendary in Saskatchewan. Long before the famous hockey playing Sutter brothers came along in the 1980s, there were six hockey playing Bentley brothers in total: Jack, Roy, Wyatt, Reg, Doug, and Max. Jack's and Roy's careers went back as far as 1925. Doug, Max and, briefly, Reg, were the only three brothers to play in the NHL.

Based largely on Doug's recommendations, the Black Hawks scouted Max. A year later, Max Bentley joined Doug in Chicago. Using give and take plays they learned from their days skating outdoors in Saskatchewan, the brothers took Chicago by storm. The brothers played with many linemates, but as a twosome, they were always dangerous.

December 4, 1941, was one spectacular evening. The Black Hawks walloped the Montreal Canadiens 9–2. Doug had a hat trick in the game, and Max assisted on all three goals. On January 28, 1943, they had one of the finest nights a line has ever had in the NHL. The Hawks beat the Rangers 10–1, and the Bentleys combined for 13 points. Doug had two goals and four assists; Max had four goals and three assists. That season turned out to be one of Doug's finest. He scored 33 goals and accumulated 73 points to win his first and only Art Ross Trophy as the NHL's leading scorer. Max was no slouch either, finishing in third place, just three points behind his brother.

When World War II started, Max enlisted. Many wondered how Doug would handle his brother's absence. It turned out that there was nothing to worry about. In fact, Doug had his finest season in 1943–1944, finishing second in NHL scoring with 38 goals and 77 points. In the 1943–1944 playoffs, he added another 12 points in nine games and led the Black Hawks to the Stanley Cup finals, where they lost to the powerful Montreal Canadiens.

At the start of the 1944–1945 season, Doug's career took a rather bizarre turn. The Hawks were travelling to Canada to play an exhibition game. On their return, Doug was refused permission to join the Black Hawks because of military travel restrictions. Bentley spent the entire 1944–1945 season out of the NHL and remained at home in Saskatchewan. During his year off, Bentley tended the family farm and served as a player-coach for a local senior hockey team called the Laura Beavers, with future Maple Leafs' goalie, Johnny Bower.

Doug and Max returned to the team for the 1945–1946 season and were placed on a line with a speedy winger named Bill Mosienko. Together, the small, speedy trio flourished, and because of their colt-like moves on the ice, they became known as the Pony Line.

"I don't know who gave us the name, but it felt nice and it stuck," said Max. "We had so much fun playing together. [Doug and Bill] were the best I ever saw, the fastest. They had different styles. When we were coming up to the other team's blue line, Mosie [Mosienko] liked me to pass him the puck before he hit the defence and he'd carry it around them. With Doug, he wanted me to dump the puck between the two defencemen and he'd swoop around and pick it up. We used to talk about ideas like that."

During that same season, the Bentley brothers made history. Doug and Max's older brother, Reg, was called up from the minors. Naturally, he was put on a line with Doug and Max. It was the first time three brothers played as a complete forward line. Reg's stay with the Black Hawks was brief. He played in just 11 games before being returned to the minors.

"Reg liked his fun," said Max. "He'd rather shoot pool the afternoon of the game when he should have been resting. He'd be ready to sleep by the time the game was starting. He didn't last."

Although the Black Hawks had won the Stanley Cup in 1938, the team was at the beginning of a tailspin that would see them fail to win another Stanley Cup until 1961, the team's last championship to date. The Hawks relied heavily on the

Pony Line and failed to surround the trio with any talent. The team was lousy in goal and on defence, and their second and third lines were ineffective. As a result, opponents knew that if they played aggressively against the Pony Line, they could effectively shut down the entire team.

"That's where the speed comes in," noted Max. "We had to keep moving fast all the time. We had to have our legs in shape."

After the Black Hawks missed the playoffs in 1946–1947, Tobin decided that he was going to have to trade his biggest commodity, Max Bentley. Before he did, Tobin actually approached Doug and Max about his intentions.

"Mr. Tobin called me and Doug into his office for a talk this one day," remembered Max. "I'd heard rumours about a trade but I never dreamed it'd be me. Mr. Tobin said it was up to myself whether I went or not. He said it'd help Chicago a lot, getting five top players like that. So I thought, well, I'll go [even though] it made me feel like I lost my right arm."

Doug wasn't thrilled with the idea of trading his brother, but admitted that if it would help improve the team, "it might be the best thing for the two of us."

A few days later, Max was traded to the Toronto Maple Leafs for five players: Bud Poile, Bob Goldham, Gaye Stewart, Gus Bodnar, and Ernie Dickens. The Leafs won three Stanley Cups in the next four years, but the trade did little for the Black Hawks.

Some hockey observers felt that Doug's career would

Doug Bentley

collapse without his brother beside him. However, he continued to flourish and finished among the league's top scorers.
The year Max left, Doug finished third in NHL scoring. The
following season, 1948–1949, he was even better, finishing
second to teammate Roy Conacher in league scoring, with
66 points. Doug did just fine without Max.

Unfortunately, Doug's achievements were often lost because of the mediocre team around him. Between 1945 and 1958, the Black Hawks only made the playoffs twice. Although he played 566 regular season games, Doug only participated in 23 playoff games during his career. Much of the blame for the team's failings rested on the shoulders of Bill Tobin.

"Tobin is so cheap," Leafs owner, Conn Smythe, once said, "that he wouldn't pay 10 cents to see the Statue of Liberty take a swan dive into New York Harbour."

However, Doug's accomplishments didn't go entirely unnoticed. In 1950, he was awarded the Half-Century Award as Chicago's best player by the Chicago newspaper *Herald American.*

Despite their stoic reactions, in truth, Max's trade to Toronto had broken the brothers' hearts. However, no one was more bothered by the trade than their father, Bill.

"[My dad] heard it on the radio," recalled Max. "He wanted me and Doug to stay together."

Bill Bentley was a strong family man and liked his children to be close. He wondered if his two famous sons would ever play together again. When Doug retired in 1952, and Max followed a year later, it seemed that Bill Bentley's dream would be unfulfilled.

During the summer of 1953, something miraculous occurred. New York Rangers' manager, Frank Boucher, approached Max about coming out of retirement.

"When I quit hockey in 1953," said Max, "I really was serious about it. I had played a lot of good hockey in Toronto, but missed Doug. Then Frank Boucher started asking if I'd play just one more season with New York. He kept hiking his offer until I accepted. The money was too good to turn down."

The Bentley signing created a buzz in New York. "Our town has its biggest hockey hero in years," said Jimmy Powers in the *New York Daily News*.

Max alone couldn't help the Rangers, though. "There were many times that he sat," wrote hockey columnist, Stan Fischler, "head hung low, white towel draped over his neck, at the end of the bench...."

Still, Max's return was so impressive that a Ranger official approached Boucher about bringing back another Bentley ... Doug. "If Doug can stand up," said the official, "he must be better than most of these kids we've got."

Boucher agreed, but he also realized that unlike Max, Doug had been away from the game for a year coaching minor hockey. The more Boucher thought about it, the more convinced he was that it was worth the risk. However, when Boucher called the owner of the Saskatoon Quakers team that Bentley was coaching, Boucher's request was refused.

It was the middle of December, and the season was half over. The Rangers were battling the Bruins for the final playoff spot. A desperate Boucher decided to get tough. He called the Saskatoon owner back and threatened to pull all Rangers-owned players from the team. Considering the Rangers owned most of the players on the roster, the Quakers would barely have been able to ice a team. Boucher then offered to replace Doug with Frankie Eddolls, a former NHL defenceman, who had coaching potential. By mid-January, Doug Bentley was on his way to New York.

Doug was doubtful from the beginning. "I was only doing spot playing with the Quakers. On top of that, I had been having a bad time with my nerves. I didn't think the NHL would help that condition. But Boucher kept after me and finally, he offered me the biggest money I ever got in my life, even in my best days with the Black Hawks. The money did it. That and the fact that I knew I could help Max."

Things did not begin well. Doug was scheduled to debut on Wednesday, January 21, 1954. The Rangers were taking on the fourth place Boston Bruins. The Rangers only trailed the Bruins by two points. It was a pivotal game. However, Doug's flight didn't leave Saskatchewan until late Tuesday night. Just as they were about take off, Doug realized that he had left his skates at the arena.

"They had to hold the flight while I went back to get them," said Doug.

The flight finally left, and an exhausted Bentley arrived in New York on Wednesday afternoon. By then, the New York media was carrying the story that the Bentley brothers would be reunited that night against Boston. The buzz about their reunion didn't help Doug's nerves.

"I was afraid I'd make a fool of myself. I was as nervous as a kitten … must have walked up and down the dressing room at least 100 times."

Finally, the game started. Doug's doubts faded fast.

"Once the people started to holler for us," said Doug, "I knew that was it. I knew we'd really go. I knew because right off the bat I could tell that Max hadn't forgotten any of his tricks — or mine either."

Just 12:29 into the opening period, he scored. A few minutes later, Max assisted on a power play goal; then Doug set up a third goal to give the Rangers an early 3–0 lead. The Bruins quickly countered with two of their own to make the score 3–2 after one period.

Early in the second period, the brothers struck again, in vintage Bentley style.

"We criss-crossed a couple of times on our way to their blue line," said Doug. "Then I fed it to Max and he put it right in."

Max was overwhelmed after the goal, and when he returned to the bench, he placed his arm on Doug's shoulder and said, "Same old Doug. You're skating the same, handing off the same, and fooling 'em the same."

A few minutes later, they did it again, this time setting up Camille Henry's goal. After the second period, the Rangers were up 6–3.

With just five minutes remaining and the Rangers up 7–3, the fans began to call for the Bentley boys. Coach Frank

Patrick heard their cries and sent the brothers out with Edgar Laprade. As Stan Fischler tells it, "Flanked by the brothers, Laprade swiftly crossed the centre red line, then skimmed a pass to Doug on the left who just as quickly sent it back to Laprade as he crossed the Boston blue line. By now, only one Bruin defenceman was back, trying to intercept the anticipated centre slot pass from Laprade to Max speeding along the right side. Laprade tantalized the Boston player, almost handed him the puck, and when he lunged for it, Edgar flipped it to Max, who was moving on a direct line for the right goalpost. Meanwhile, Laprade had burst ahead on a direct line for the left goalpost, ready for a return pass. Both goalie Jim Henry and the defenceman — and possibly even Laprade — expected Max to relay the puck back to Edgar and so Henry began edging toward the other side of the net as Max faked and faked and faked the pass but continued to move toward the goal until, without even shooting, he calmly eased it into the right corner while Henry stood there mesmerized by the Bentley magic."

"It was like a dream," said Doug. "Everything we did turned out right."

The Rangers won the game 8–3. Doug finished with one goal and three assists, while Max chipped in with two goals and two assists. It was their finest night since their 13-point performance in January 1943.

The New York media were ecstatic in their praise. "To say that the reunion was a success is a weak understatement," wrote Joe Nichols of the *New York Times.* "The Bentleys frolicked like a couple of kids out skylarking."

"I've been covering hockey since 1928," wrote Jimmy Powers of the *Daily News,* "and this game, to me, was one of the most thrilling of all time. I know, because at the end I was so hoarse from cheering, I couldn't talk."

Inside the dressing room after the game, Max sat crying.

"He's crying for happiness," said Doug. "He's tickled because we finally played together again … and so am I."

The performance convinced Doug to remain with the Rangers for the rest of the season. Unfortunately, the Bentley's thrilling return would remain the high point of the season. The Bruins finished six points ahead of the Rangers. Playoffs or not, the Bentley boys gave Rangers' fans an evening to remember.

"My father said at the time that we shouldn't let them break us up," said Doug about his father's reaction to Max being traded to the Leafs. "And he was right. All I could say after that reunion was that I wished we could have turned the clock back 10 years. But we couldn't."

Both Doug and Max retired following the 1953–1954 season. Incredibly, Doug made an eight-game comeback in 1961 with the Los Angeles Blades of the Western Hockey League. The 45 year old played on a line with the NHL's first black player, Willie O'Ree. Doug was voted into the Hockey Hall of Fame in 1964, and Max followed two years later.

Chapter 4
Ted Lindsay

If there is a single picture that sums up Ted Lindsay's 16-year NHL career with the Detroit Red Wings and Chicago Black Hawks, it's the night he held his stick like a rifle and pretended to shoot at the Maple Leaf Garden's crowd.

Prior to a 1956 playoff game against the Toronto Maple Leafs, an angry Toronto fan had threatened the lives of Lindsay and linemate, Gordie Howe. Although Lindsay wasn't worried, a detachment of plain-clothed policemen was assigned to escort Lindsay and Howe to the game.

The threat had thrown the Wings off their game. They played hesitantly and found themselves down 4–2 with less than 12 minutes remaining in the game. Then Lindsay and Howe went to work. Howe struck first at 9:11 of the third period when he fired a pass from defencemen, Red Kelly, past Leafs' goalie, Harry Lumley, to bring the Wings to within a goal. Five minutes later, Lindsay tied the game with a low shot from 30 feet out.

The game headed into overtime, but not for long. Just 4:22 into the extra frame, Lindsay slammed home a pass from Bob Goldham to give the Wings a commanding 3–0 lead in the series. After scoring the goal, the tempestuous Lindsay circled the ice, aimed his stick like a machine gun, and began firing imaginary bullets into the crowd. No one was going to threaten Ted Lindsay.

He only stood five foot, seven inches, but there were none tougher than Ted Lindsay. As a man and player, "Terrible Ted" (as he was nicknamed because of his vicious temper) or "Scarface" (for his many stitches) backed down from no one. Throughout his career, Lindsay battled anyone who got in his way, from opponents, referees, coaches, and managers to fans, policemen, teammates, and even the NHL itself.

"A little guy has to have plenty of self-confidence, maybe even seem cocky," said Lindsay in 1957. "I had the idea that I should beat up every player I tangled with, and I'm still not convinced it wasn't a good idea. What are you going to do when some guy starts giving it to you — skate away? You wouldn't last five games."

Lindsay had 1,808 penalty minutes during his career. His short temper led to many nasty altercations, like the famous night in 1951 when Lindsay knocked Toronto's Wild

Bill Ezinicki unconscious with a flurry of stick chops and punches. Ezinicki ended up with 19 stitches, two black eyes, and a broken nose. Lindsay had three stitches, a black eye, and couldn't open his right hand for more than a week.

"He's sneaky," said Maple Leaf defenceman, Jim Thomson, in 1957. "You've got to keep your eyes open all the time or he'll cut your heart out. He can be the friendly fellow off the ice, but when they drop that puck, look out."

"That Lindsay!" Maurice "Rocket" Richard once said, "Oh, he used to make me sore."

There was more to Lindsay than fighting though. He could also play hockey. Lindsay scored 851 points in 1,068 games. Playing on the famous Production Line, Lindsay and linemates, Gordie Howe and Sid Abel, dominated the NHL between 1948 and 1955. During that time, the Red Wings won seven straight league titles and four Stanley Cups. Lindsay was also named an all-star nine times. When he retired, Lindsay was considered the greatest left winger to play the game.

Lindsay, the youngest of nine children, was born with hockey in his blood. His father, Bert, played senior hockey at McGill University in Montreal. In 1906, he moved to Renfrew and played in the Ottawa Valley senior league. In 1909, Lindsay was the starting goalie for the Renfrew Creamery Kings when they joined the newly formed National Hockey Association. (The Kings were later nicknamed "The Millionaires" because of their star-studded roster that included Cyclone Taylor, Lester Patrick, and Newsy Lalonde.)

After following Lester Patrick out west, Lindsay starred for four seasons with the Victoria Aristocrats. Two years later, he returned to the NHA with the Montreal Wanderers. Bert was with the Wanderers when they became one of the founding members of the NHL in 1917. Unfortunately, the team folded the same year, when their arena burned down. The following year, Lindsay was signed by the defending Stanley Cup champions, the Toronto Arenas. He played one year with the Arenas before retiring. After his hockey career, Bert worked for a trucking firm. When the company closed in 1933, Bert moved the family up north to Kirkland Lake, Ontario, where he found work managing the local rink.

"My first pair of skates was given to me by a neighbour named Mrs. Brady, who gave me her husband Tom's skates," remembers Ted Lindsay. "They were naturally too big for me but I put them on and in my little imagination, I would skate from one end of the rink to the other and across the rink in her backyard. Every second or third home had a rink in their backyard. … My Dad decided I would get a pair of skates of my own."

During his first day out on the ice, young Ted suffered the first of his many injuries. While struggling to maintain his balance, Ted hit a crack and fell face first into the ice. He broke two teeth. He was so scared that his mother would stop him from skating again that he didn't tell her about the teeth. He even developed a way of smiling without moving his upper lip from his teeth. Eventually, the teeth became infected, and he had to have a permanent plate installed. Fortunately, he was still allowed to skate.

In high school, Lindsay starred for the Holy Name Juveniles and led them to two Ontario championships. Lindsay then turned down offers from junior teams in Galt and St. Catharines to join St. Michael's School in Toronto. When St. Mikes lost the 1944 OHL finals to the Oshawa Generals, Lindsay was invited by the opponents to replace an injured player for the Memorial Cup final. Lindsay scored nine points in seven games and helped the Generals win the national championship.

If not for an injury, Lindsay would have been one of the Toronto Maple Leafs. When someone recommended Lindsay to Leafs' coach, Hap Day, he sent assistant manager Frank Selke to see a St. Mike's game. However, when Selke showed up, Lindsay wasn't playing.

"I played for St. Mike's, and the first game I played against the Toronto Marlboros, I got injured," Lindsay told writer, Kevin Shea. "My calf got cut. Gus Mortson was playing defence and future Leafs' player, Jimmy Thomson, was playing for the Marlboros. He was going down the ice and Gus put his hip out. Jimmy was a big guy and was skating hard and he spun Gus around on one skate like he was a figure skater and the back of Gus's skate punctured my calf muscle just back of the shin pad. I ended up right on the ice with nothing but blood all around me."

Selke thought that St. Mike's swift skating winger, Joe

Sadler, was the player he was supposed to be watching. Sadler had a strong game, and Selke put him on the Leafs' negotiation list. Meanwhile, when Lindsay returned, his play suffered and no NHL teams were scouting him. After the Christmas break, his play began to improve.

"I was scoring goals, we were winning games, and I was getting into fights and winning more than I was losing," said Lindsay. "One night, I came out of the Arena in Hamilton and a man in the intersection said, 'You Ted Lindsay?' I said, 'Yes sir.' He said, 'I'm Carson Cooper, chief scout of the Detroit Red Wings. Did you ever think about playing pro?' My eyes went wide and I said, 'Yes sir.' He said, 'I'm going to put you on our list.'"

The Wings were so impressed with Lindsay that they invited him to the Red Wings' 1944–1945 training camp. He was then offered a two-year deal that included a no-minor-league clause, guaranteeing he'd play in the NHL. Lindsay's first two seasons were average, but prior to his 1946–1947 season, he was placed on a line with Sid Abel and a young rookie named Gordie Howe. The new line clicked immediately, and Lindsay flourished with 27 goals. Within a year, the Production Line, as they were called, began to dominate the league. In 1948–1949, Lindsay led the NHL in goals, and the following season, the Production Line finished 1–2–3 in league scoring, with Lindsay winning the Art Ross Trophy.

When Abel was traded to the Chicago Black Hawks in 1952, Lindsay was named captain of the Red Wings.

"He's my kind of hockey player," said Detroit general manager and coach Jack Adams, after naming Lindsay captain. "Lindsay is captain because Lindsay is a fighter and a leader. He's a player who never quits himself and can stir his team up in the dressing room and on the ice."

Gordie Howe once noted, "Ted played every game as if it was the seventh game of the Stanley Cup final."

Lindsay's play was once described as "that of a little rooster strutting around the barnyard looking for trouble." Lindsay could skate and stickhandle well, but his forte was checking. No one worked harder along the boards and in the corners. Lindsay used his stick, elbow, or body, whatever it took to get the puck free.

"If the player you were trying to take the puck away from knew you were going to give him a little shot — a bodycheck, or an elbow, or a little stick on his body — his concentration would be broken," Lindsay told writer Frank Orr.

While the Red Wings loved Lindsay's aggression on the ice, they weren't enthralled by his independent behaviour off it. Jack Adams was an old-school manager who believed that players should follow his commands, no questions asked. Lindsay wasn't like that. He was independent and smart.

"They don't think we have minds of our own," Lindsay once said of the NHL owners. "They treat us like we are little babies."

If Lindsay didn't agree with a trade or a contract, he would let Adams know. On many occasions, Lindsay was even heard speaking out against Adams' instructions on the bench. Needless to say, Adams didn't like Lindsay's fearless attitude, but he was more disturbed that Lindsay had enormous influence on the team. While most veterans went out of their way to make life awful for rookies, Lindsay was the opposite. He was friendly, encouraging, and protective. He not only spoke to the younger players, but he often took them out for dinner and beers. He went out of his way to make them feel comfortable.

Lindsay even forced the team to go out together every Monday. "You had to go," recalled former Red Wing trainer Lefty Wilson, to Gordie Howe biographer, Roy MacSkimming. "You couldn't get out of it. If you didn't go, you'd pay anyways. Lindsay'd come along and say, 'Where were you last night?' And you'd have to pay whatever it cost, 10 bucks or something. And you'd pay up."

Lindsay's relationship with Adams went from bad to worse in 1955. Despite winning the 1955 Stanley Cup, Adams stunned the hockey world when he made two massive trades. First, he sent Glen Skov, Tony Leswick, Johnny Wilson, and Benny Woit to Chicago for Dave Creighton, Bucky Hollingsworth, John McCormack, and Jerry Toppazzini. Five days later, Adams traded all-star goalie Terry Sawchuk, along with Marcel Bonin, Lorne Davis, and Vic Stasiuk to the Boston Bruins for Gilles Boisvert, Real Chevrefils, Norm Corcoran, Warren Godfrey, and Ed Sandford. In less than a week, Adams had traded half of the Stanley Cup lineup from the previous spring.

Ted Lindsay

An angry Lindsay broke an unwritten code by publicly criticizing the Sawchuk trade. "We had Glenn Hall coming up, so Sawchuk was expendable. But the only place we had a weakness was on defence. If Adams had traded Sawchuk to Montreal, we could have got Doug Harvey or Tom Johnson."

Just before the 1956 season opened, Adams had his

revenge on Lindsay by announcing to the media that Lindsay's four-year tenure as captain had ended. When asked why, Adams referred to a previously unheard of team policy of rotating the captaincy.

"Shifting the responsibility to another will help ease the tension on Ted and will help us develop for the future," said Adams.

Lindsay didn't learn about the move until he read the papers the following day.

"It was pathetic how Adams destroyed the team," said a still bitter Lindsay. "Of course, there was an uproar about it. We won seven championships in a row. We should have won seven Stanley Cups."

Lindsay's protective nature extended beyond the Red Wings. When he and Montreal Canadiens' defenceman Doug Harvey were appointed to the NHL Pension Society Board, Lindsay quickly learned that something was not right with the distribution of pensions. When he or Harvey tried to ask questions, they were given vague responses. After one meeting, Harvey and Lindsay went for beers and discussed their salaries, which no one did at the time. Soon the two men were calculating various figures, and they realized that the owners had been feeding them a line. Hockey was highly profitable, and the players were being cheated out of their fair share.

During a pre-game skate of the all-star game in October 1956, Lindsay approached Harvey about forming a player's association. Harvey agreed to help Lindsay, and soon they also had the support of other captains, including Bill Gadsby of the Rangers, Gus Mortson of the Black Hawks, Fern Flaman of the Bruins, and Jimmy Thomson of the Maple Leafs.

On February 11, 1957, Lindsay, Harvey, and the other players held a press conference in New York announcing the formation of the National Hockey League Players' Association (NHLPA). During the conference, Lindsay said that the association "will promote, foster, and protect the best interests of NHL players."

The owners were outraged by the move. Toronto owner, Conn Smythe, called his team's representative, Jimmy Thomson, "a traitor" and sent him to the Leafs' farm team before trading him six months later to Chicago. Initially, Jack Adams, Red Wings' general manager, said nothing about Lindsay's role in the NHLPA. That soon changed. Despite having his finest season in 1956–1957, Lindsay was accused, by Adams, of having complacent and undisciplined play.

On July 24, 1957, the battle finally ended when Adams stunned the hockey world by trading Lindsay and goalie Glenn Hall, to the lowly Chicago Black Hawks for Johnny Wilson, Forbes Kennedy, Hank Bassen, and Bill Preston. From a hockey perspective, it was a ludicrous trade. Lindsay and Hall, who had just come off all-star seasons, were traded for four mediocre players.

Red Wings' fans were livid about the deal and jammed the Detroit Olympia switchboard with calls of protest. For his part, Lindsay once again did something no player had done before. He called his own press conference.

"I wanted to close my hockey career in Detroit," Lindsay stated during the conference, "but derogatory remarks about myself and my family showed me that the personal resentment on the part of the Detroit general manager would make it impossible for me to continue playing in Detroit."

Lindsay spent three seasons in Chicago. He never matched his point totals from his Detroit days, but Lindsay's leadership provided an important spark to the young, struggling Black Hawks team. After a decade of losing, Lindsay helped the Black Hawks return to respectability. Meanwhile, without Lindsay, the Red Wings slipped from first place to dead last during the same three-year period.

Adam's dismantling of the Red Wings frustrated Lindsay for years. "I've always said that we were a dynasty — there's no doubt about it," Lindsay told Kevin Shea of the Hockey Hall of Fame. "Montreal interrupted that, but it never would have been interrupted if we didn't have a less than competent general manager in Jack Adams. Mr. Adams traded nine players away from our championship team. That's 50 percent! That destroyed the nucleus of our team."

Lindsay and former Red Wings' teammate Marty Pavelich had been involved in a successful plastics business for years, another activity that infuriated Adams. However, the trade to Chicago made it difficult for Lindsay to take care of his business and play hockey. Although Pavelich was taking care of the business, Lindsay felt guilty about leaving his partner with all the responsibility. "I always seemed to be looking at the clock, checking the weather, thinking about the flight home."

It didn't help that Lindsay didn't feel at home in Chicago. "I went to Chicago for three years but I was never a Black Hawk." Lindsay recalled. "I was treated well by the fans and by management, but I only had mediocre years. I still had a Red Wing on my forehead, on my backside and over my heart."

Following a sub-par 1959–1960 season, Lindsay retired from the NHL, having played 999 games. "I don't want to wind up as an athletic bum," Lindsay stated upon his retirement. "When the fire is out, it's time for an athlete to quit. To play any longer would be taking their money under false pretences."

Once again, Lindsay displayed an honesty and integrity that was, and remains, rare among athletes.

In 1964, Lindsay reunited with Sid Abel and Gordie Howe for an old-timers' game. Lindsay played so well that Abel, who was then the coach of the Red Wings, approached Lindsay about returning to the team.

"When I picked myself off the floor," said Lindsay, "I realized Sid was serious."

Lindsay took a few days to consider Abel's offer. After discussing it with his wife, Pat, and business partner, Marty Pavelich, Lindsay immediately ignored their advice and went to the Wings' training camp. He worked out for a month with the team, but his possible return remained a well-kept secret.

What motivated Lindsay's return? It wasn't for money or personal records. "I just had the desire to finish off my career in a Red Wing's sweater," Lindsay said.

The day before opening night of the 1964–1965 season, Abel asked Lindsay if he was ready to play. Lindsay wasn't sure and asked for another 10 days to train.

Abel said, "The only way you're going to find out is to play."

Lindsay agreed and signed a one-year contract.

That night, Detroit fans got the surprise of their lives when Lindsay was introduced into a spotlight in the darkened Olympia arena. Before the public address announcer called Lindsay's name, the arena exploded into a roar of applause at the sight of their former captain. Ted Lindsay was home.

Reaction to Lindsay's comeback was mostly negative. NHL president, Clarence Campbell, called it "a black day for hockey." Campbell felt that if a 39 year old man could return to the world's fastest sport after four years away, it would hurt the image of the NHL.

As was typical for Lindsay, he made his critics eat their words. It turned out to be an amazing year for both Lindsay and the Red Wings. Lindsay scored 14 goals and 14 assists and helped the Red Wings finish in first place. Lindsay's achievements led Campbell to reverse his initial criticism.

"This is one of the most amazing feats in professional sport," Campbell stated in a 1965 publicity release. "I know I was among the many knowledgeable hockey people who expressed skepticism ... but I was wrong."

It was indeed a remarkable achievement. Many players had come out of retirement after a year, but no one had been out for four years and returned to play at such a high level. At the end of the year, Lindsay retired for good.

Lindsay couldn't even go into the Hockey Hall of Fame quietly. On June 17, 1966, Lindsay received a letter that he was being inducted into the Hall of Fame. Near the end of the letter, it noted: "The Luncheon will be strictly a 'stag' affair." Lindsay politely refused to participate in the male-only affair.

"If my family can't share in this, I won't go," Lindsay said. "I have my principles."

The next year, the policy was changed to permit both men and women to the event.

Throughout the 70s and 80s, Lindsay remained connected with hockey. In 1973, he was the colour commentator for the NBC game of the week, and in 1976, he was hired as general manager of the Red Wings. As GM, Lindsay promised to bring "aggressive hockey" back to town.

Unfortunately, Lindsay had limited success as a manager and, for a few games, as coach. To no one's surprise, Lindsay was a difficult man to deal with as a manager. He had disagreements with players, team owners, and the NHL.

Ironically, he was often in the headlines battling with Alan Eagleson, the head of the NHL Player's Association (NHLPA). While Lindsay still supported the NHLPA, he believed that Eagleson "lacked integrity."

In a 1976 *Toronto Star* article, Lindsay even suggested, without mentioning Eagleson's name, that the players get rid of their leader. "The players' association," said Lindsay "should be taking a strong stand on things happening right now instead of being used to help one man."

The "hero" label has been used and abused in our society. Ted Lindsay, though, is a hero. On the ice he was fearless. Off-ice, he wasn't afraid to speak out about injustices leveled against himself and others.

"I don't do anything to agitate or irritate people or look for recognition," Lindsay said in 1977. "I just do what I believe in."

Chapter 5
Dickie Moore

e're thinking of trading you," Montreal Canadiens' general manager, Frank Selke, told his star left winger, Dickie Moore, in May 1963.

"No, nobody trades me," replied Moore. "I quit."

Moore walked out of the office. The next day, the Montreal papers announced that Dickie Moore had retired from hockey.

It was an unceremonious and humiliating end for a man who had given so much to the team. Moore had overcome injuries that would have ended the careers of most players. Moore's courage was remarkable, and his ability and desire to overcome countless physical setbacks was an inspiration to his teammates. Most incredibly, Moore won a scoring championship in 1958 while playing with a broken wrist.

"His alleged handicaps," wrote Milt Dunnell of the *Toronto Star,* "have included three shoulder separations, perennial miseries in both knees, broken feet, cracked knuckles, fractured wrists, [and] cuts and abrasions too numerous to mention."

How bad were Moore's injuries? During a Montreal Canadiens' training camp in Victoria in the early 60s, *Montreal Gazette* reporter Red Fisher took a walk with Moore. As they were walking, Fisher kept hearing a loud cracking sound.

"What's that funny sound?" Fisher asked Moore.

"What sound?"

"Don't you hear it? That cracking noise we've been hearing for the last few minutes," Fisher told Moore.

"Oh, that," Moore said with a laugh. "Those are my knees. Every step I take."

They didn't come much tougher than Montreal Canadiens' left winger, Dickie Moore. Despite racking up 608 points and six Stanley Cups in 14 seasons, Moore's outstanding play was often overshadowed on a team that featured Rocket Richard, Bernie Geoffrion, Jean Beliveau, Jacques Plante, and Doug Harvey. Even as a left winger, Moore was often overlooked by the more visible exploits of Ted Lindsay and, later, Frank Mahovlich and Bobby Hull. In truth, Moore may have been the real inspiration behind the great Canadiens teams of the 1950s.

Dickie Moore

"I really wanted to be a hockey player from five years old," Moore remembered. "At seven years old, I broke my right leg very badly. It was a bicycle accident. I had a cast from my foot right up to the top of my leg. … The muscle in my thigh never developed. I was nervous that I wouldn't be able to skate the next year. It came around, and I was able to participate in all the sports."

Dickie Moore grew up in a large family of nine boys and one girl in the rough English-speaking Montreal suburb of Park Extension.

"Our family built a rink right beside our house. We used to bring the firetruck in and they'd water the rink for us. All the kids in the area used to come and skate there. My brothers taught me to skate and taught me the game."

While most Montreal kids grew up cheering for the Canadiens, Moore was a Toronto Maple Leafs fan as a boy.

"It was all radio broadcasting when I was growing up," Moore said. "I latched on to Gordie Drillon, who was playing for the Toronto Maple Leafs at that time. I used to try to copy him on the ice, on the street — wherever we could play hockey. It was a lot of fun."

During his minor hockey days, Moore had the reputation of being a hot-tempered kid who was headed for a tough life. Unhappy with the Park Extension Hockey Association, Moore started his own team at age 13.

"We used to get second-hand equipment from the [Montreal] Forum," says Moore. "I even got sticks from the

Forum. Our team went to the city finals and did a hell of a job."

Although he made many coaches anxious, Moore was a good player who was regarded early on as a "can't miss" NHL prospect. At age 15, Moore joined the Montreal Junior Royals, and in his first full season in 1948–1949, he helped the Royals become the first Memorial Cup champions from Quebec. Moore's play soon attracted NHL attention, and he almost became a Toronto Maple Leaf.

"A scout from the Maple Leafs," remembered Moore, "asked me if I was interested in joining the Leafs. I said, 'Sure.' He said, 'We'll get in touch with you.'"

Word got back to Canadiens' manager Frank Selke that the Leafs were after Moore.

"I was working at the CPR [Canadian Pacific Railway] at the time and Selke called me up and said, 'Can I see you?' I said, 'I can't get away from work.' I had a feeling why he wanted to see me and I was waiting for the Leafs to call me."

When the Leafs didn't call, Moore signed with Montreal.

The following season, Moore moved from the Junior Royals to the Junior Canadiens and won another Memorial Cup championship. After a second season with the Junior Canadiens, Moore received an invitation to attend the Canadiens' training camp. Things didn't go quite the way Moore had hoped.

"I tried my best but I could see that I wasn't in their immediate plans."

Selke told Moore that he was being assigned to the Senior Montreal Royals team. Moore initially refused to join the Royals. However, when Selke assured him that he would join the Canadiens by Christmas, Moore reluctantly agreed.

Selke kept his word, and Moore joined the Canadiens in December 1951. On a line with Rocket Richard and Elmer Lach, Moore was an instant success, scoring 33 points in his first 33 games.

"This kid Moore could give us the spark that we need to revive this club," coach Dick Irvin said at the time. "He can't skate much and I don't know whether he can handle the puck. I do know he's a competitor."

Unfortunately, injuries soon put a stop to Moore's impressive NHL debut. During his first three seasons in the NHL, Moore missed 112 games.

"First it was my knee, then my shoulder," said Moore. "The most painful injury I ever had was a smashed collarbone. I made a nice pass, a very nice pass. It was so nice that I couldn't resist watching it go to my wingman. That is about all I did see because Gordie Hudson crashed me from the other side and I went into the boards with my shoulder harness knocked up around my neck."

Injuries weren't Moore's only problem. The temper that he showed as a junior player continued to appear occasionally in the NHL. One night in New York, an agitated Moore was skating around Madison Square Garden hitting every

Ranger in sight. Soon, it looked like Moore was going to fight the entire Rangers' team. Finally, he picked Rangers' captain, Red Sullivan. Moore smashed Sullivan with his stick and belted him with a flurry of punches.

"He used to go ding-dong like that all the time, you know, wild," said Ranger's defenceman Bill Gadsby.

"He was a wild man," remembered teammate, Jean Beliveau, "and on more than one occasion went up in the stands after long-distance tormenters."

"When he came to Madison Square Garden," remembered hockey writer Stan Fischler, in the TV series, *Legends of Hockey,* "the fans chanted 'GET MOORE! GET MOORE! GET MOORE!' They didn't chant Get Richard! Get Geoffrion! or Get Harvey! and that said everything you had to know about Dickie Moore as a competitor."

"The boos didn't bother me a bit," said Moore. "As long as I knew I played a good game. I didn't carry any grudges from one season to the next, either. But during the year, you had to get a guy if he got you. I didn't go out of my way to get anybody; they were always looking for me."

Moore's antics occasionally bothered Frank Selke. After Moore's antics cost the Canadiens a game, Selke told the press, "We didn't play well, and as for Moore, he should be in Hollywood with an act like that."

By 1955, the injuries were beginning to frustrate Moore. "There were days when I thought I'd chuck it all and go into something more secure."

Dickie Moore

The Canadiens also grew impatient and began offering Moore to other teams around the league. Ironically, during his third year, Moore only missed three games. However, all season he played with a shoulder that popped out of place every few games. Selke had seen enough and figured Moore was finished as a player. He was ready to trade him to the first buyer. When Selke couldn't find a buyer, he was forced to keep Moore.

Moore's luck began to change during the 1955–1956 season. He only scored 50 points that season, but he played a full 70 game season. Playing the entire season seemed to be the cure for Moore's ailments. His confidence soared, and he found his rhythm. Perhaps the biggest influence on Moore's play was the team's new coach, Toe Blake.

Following the infamous "Richard Riot" in March 1955 when Montreal fans rioted in the streets of Montreal in protest of the suspension of Rocket Richard, Frank Selke had decided that the team needed a new coach, one who could control Richard's fiery temper. After the 1954–1955 season, Selke called Irvin into his office and said, "Look, Dick, you can't coach this team any longer. It's all very well to keep a team full of fight. But there's a limit to that, too. And I don't think you know the limit."

Soon after, Selke hired former Canadien captain and Richard linemate, Toe Blake, to take over. The coaching change did a world of good for Moore.

"Dick Irvin and I didn't get along too well," adds Moore.

"When Toe became coach, I was elated. He kept me on the team. I was lucky to have a guy who believed in me."

That season under Blake, the Canadiens won the first of their five Stanley Cups.

With three months left in the 1957–1958 season, Moore was finally healthy and having his best season to date. Moore was battling with teammate, Henri Richard, and the Rangers' Andy Bathgate for the NHL scoring lead. Then one night in Detroit, the Wings' Marcel Pronovost hip-checked Moore.

"My stick," remembered Moore, "jabbed into him and I fractured my wrist. The wrist was hurting me, but I kept on playing."

X-rays later showed a fracture. The doctors felt it was best that Moore have an operation immediately to fix the break and perhaps return in time for the playoffs. Moore wasn't so sure.

"Maybe you could put a cast on my arm?" he asked the doctors.

Moore was desperate. The seven-year veteran had been hampered by injuries since joining the Canadiens in 1951. This was only his third injury-free season. The Canadiens had already been very patient with Moore, but another setback might mean the end of his career.

Moore chose the cast, but he first made sure it was okay with Toe Blake.

"I felt I was hurting Henri Richard who was my centre-man. We were one and two in the scoring at the time, with

Bathgate close behind. So Toe had a meeting on the train and told Henri and a few of the other guys it was up to them. I had told 'Pocket' [Henri Richard's nickname] I thought it was unfair if I was hampering him by staying on his line, but he said it was okay. So I was pretty happy."

The team went out of their way to help Moore. His left wrist was broken, so on the power play they moved Moore over to the right side where he could "play with the one hand and catch the puck and then bring it over and shoot it or deflect it."

Incredibly, Moore finished the season with a league-leading 84 points, four more than Henri Richard. "I was never a big scorer in junior so I never expected that I would be going for a scoring championship. But when it was over, I had won."

"Who else would have finished first in scoring while wearing a cast on his left hand?" asked Frank Selke Jr.

The following season, Moore was even better. Playing in all 70 games, Moore not only won the NHL scoring championship, but he broke Gordie Howe's 1952–1953 record of 95 by one point. He followed the season with a phenomenal playoff, scoring 17 points in 11 games and leading the Canadiens to their fourth straight Stanley Cup.

Moore was satisfied, but relieved, when the scoring race was over. "It builds up on a guy. Why, for those last few weeks, Jean [Beliveau] and I kept looking over our shoulder only to see Bathgate close behind. We knew we had to keep going for those points. I was glad when it was over."

Despite his success, Moore remained uncertain about being in the limelight. "Sometimes," he said at the time, "I feel I'd rather be down about the middle of the scoring list. Then people don't notice you too much. When I first broke in I used to wonder what it would be like to lead the league. Now that I know, it sort of scares me."

The Canadiens won again in 1959–1960, but it was the end of an era. The team that had won an incredible five consecutive Stanley Cups was being dismantled. The Rocket retired following the 1959–1960 victory. All-star defenceman Doug Harvey replaced the Rocket as captain for a year before being traded to the New York Rangers in June 1961. Two years later, in 1963, goalie Jacques Plante was dealt to the Rangers for Gump Worsley.

By 1963, the Canadiens were rebuilding, and Dickie Moore was simply too rich for their blood. "I had scored 24 goals [in 1961–1962]," says Moore, "but they decided to get rid of me. My salary was up too high, and they could get a kid for $7,500. That's what I started for. My final salary with the Canadiens was $21,500." Moore was deeply hurt by the team's decision to trade him. "It was a surprise. I didn't think it was fair. I played here all my life. I just don't want to play anywhere else."

The retirement was short-lived. By September 1963, Moore had a change of heart and arrived at the Canadiens' training camp. During the first day of camp, Moore met with Selke to discuss a contract. The Canadiens were willing to sign Moore for another season. The following day, Moore and Selke met again and were close to a deal. After the meeting, Moore returned to the ice. During a drill, a young forward named Keith McCreary tried to skate past Moore. Moore immediately stretched out his left leg to slow McCreary down. As the men collided, Moore's knee got the worst of the impact. Moore went to the bench. At that moment, Moore knew he was done. The next day, he officially announced his retirement.

Once again, Moore's retirement was temporary. During the summer of 1964, the Toronto Maple Leafs drafted Moore in the 1964 Intra-League Draft.

"I got a call from King Clancy [of the Leafs]," remembered Moore, "who told me I'd been claimed by the Leafs and asked me if I'd consider playing. I said, 'Sure, I'll consider.'"

The Leafs had just won their third consecutive Stanley Cup and hoped Moore would add some leadership and offense to the young team. Moore went to Toronto to sign a contract, but told Leafs general manager Punch Imlach that he wasn't sure if he could play.

"I had shattered my kneecap that year," remembered Moore. "A grinding wheel in my shop shattered and went right into my kneecap. They wanted to remove it [the kneecap] but I said, 'You can't. I'm going back to play hockey.' I said, 'Clean it out as best you can. If I can't walk, then we'll remove the kneecap.' The doctor said, 'You're crazy,' and I said, 'Don't worry. Leave that to me.' And today, I'm still wearing that kneecap."

After a year off skates, Moore found coming back difficult and instantly regretted his decision.

An insistent Imlach said, "I signed you. I'm paying you. You're staying with me."

Moore ended up playing only 38 games for the Leafs. In the playoffs, Toronto fittingly met the Canadiens. Moore scored a goal in the first game, but Montreal won.

The following year, Toronto asked Moore to come back. However, when Imlach refused to guarantee that Moore would see much playing time, Moore refused the offer and retired for the third, but not last, time.

Moore's third retirement lasted until December 1967. He was playing old-timers' hockey once a week in Lachine, Quebec. During that time, Moore got a call from St. Louis Blues scout, Cliff Fletcher. Fletcher asked Moore if he wanted to make a comeback with the Blues. A few weeks later, St. Louis coach Scotty Bowman called Moore and asked him to join the team. Moore accepted the offer and worked hard.

"I lost 20 pounds to make the comeback, practising by myself. I picked up a youngster to act as a goaltender. I did a lot of skating and decided to go play with them."

When *Montreal Gazette* columnist Red Fisher asked Moore why he was coming back, Moore replied, "[B]ecause it's a challenge. They're paying me well and when a guy likes the game as much as I do, it's pretty hard to turn down something like this."

Moore played 27 games for St. Louis. The Blues surprised everyone in the playoffs. Led by goalie Glenn Hall and a number of ex-Montreal Canadiens, including Moore, Red Berenson, Jean-Guy Talbot, Jacques Plante, and Doug Harvey, they went to the Stanley Cup final against … the Montreal Canadiens.

Although the Blues were swept in four straight games, they put in a gutsy effort. In particular, Dickie Moore had an outstanding playoff, tallying seven goals and seven assists in 18 games.

"He was instrumental in our winning the Western Division playoffs," remembered Scotty Bowman. "In one game against the North Stars, we were down 3–0 in the third period, and he scored once and then set up two to send the game in overtime and we won it. Even at his best, I don't think Dickie ever played better than he did in the last eight minutes of that game."

Following the 1968 season, Moore's knee was finished. He retired from hockey for good. Five years later, in 1974, Dickie Moore was elected to the Hockey Hall of Fame.

Unlike many of his colleagues, Moore was prepared for a life without hockey. As early as 1958, he was involved in off-season business ventures. "I was preparing for my future," said Moore. "Let's not kid ourselves. I knew the day was going to come, that they were going to say, 'Goodbye Dick.'" When he left the game, Moore simply devoted more time to his "Dickie Moore Rentals," an equipment rental business. Today, the red and white colours of Dickie Moore's rental trailers are a familiar sight on the highways or by local skating rinks in Ottawa and Montreal.

His flashier contemporaries may have overshadowed him, but as Moore's linemate, Henri Richard, commented, his peers never forgot his courage, passion, and determination. "He was a great team man, maybe the best I have ever known. A very hard worker, he would do anything to help the team. He was the same as a person; he will sacrifice anything to help his friends."

"His heart was almost too big for his own good," wrote *Montreal Gazette* columnist Red Fisher. "Anything less than playing all-out was unacceptable. He was a grim, unflinching athlete with strong ideas of what was needed to win. If fighting was needed, [Dickie] Moore would fight."

Moore was never a pretty player. He wasn't a great skater. He wasn't the best puck handler, but there was no player who gave a more honest effort than Dickie Moore.

Chapter 6
Frank Mahovlich

I t was March 21, 1973. The Montreal Canadiens were hosting the Vancouver Canucks. It was an unimportant game in the standings. The Habs had clinched first place, and the Canucks had long been out of the playoff hunt. Yet there was anticipation in the Forum that night. It was as though the Forum faithful knew something magical was going to happen. Only four nights earlier, Montreal's Frank Mahovlich had scored his 499th career goal in Philadelphia. Montreal fans must have figured that he was saving his 500th for them.

Mahovlich's milestone motivated the Canucks. They played a tight checking game and made the Canadiens work extra hard for every foot of ice. Mahovlich almost scored the magic goal late in the first period when, incredibly, he had a breakaway from his own blue line. As he skated towards the Canuck goal with his trademark stride, the Forum fans stood and cheered. Mahovlich crossed the Canucks' blue line and approached Canucks' goalie, Dunc Wilson. Wilson didn't budge. Mahovlich was forced to shoot. As he made a slight deke to the right, he fired the puck low towards the left side of the net. However, Wilson was ready. In a flash, he blocked the shot with his arm. The fans groaned in unison.

In the second period, Mahovlich only managed two weak shots on goal. The teams headed to the dressing room with the score tied 2–2.

Early in the third period, it finally happened. As Henri Richard crossed the Canucks' blue line on the left side, he spotted Mahovlich heading towards the net. Richard fired a pass across the ice. In one fiery swoop, Mahovlich took the pass and fired the puck so hard he fell to one knee. Incredibly, the puck merely sputtered off Mahovlich's stick, slowly skidded towards the open right side of the net, and, eventually, slid across the blue line.

It was a strange goal. If he'd still been a Maple Leaf, Toronto fans probably would have booed Mahovlich for not scoring a more spectacular-looking goal. Montreal fans didn't care. They roared when the puck crossed the line and gave "The Big M" a rousing ovation. Unlike Leaf fans, Montrealers were glad to have a superstar like Mahovlich.

It was all so new for Mahovlich. In his 11 years with Toronto, no matter how hard he tried, he never seemed to do anything right. The fans, media, and owners always wanted more. Despite winning a Calder Trophy, six all-star team selections, and four Stanley Cups with Toronto, and scoring more goals than any other Maple Leafs player before him, Mahovlich was one of the most misunderstood players in team history. As Jim Hunt wrote in the 1963 *Star Weekly Magazine,* "He is the sport's only superstar who is sometimes treated like a bush-league bum." Mahovlich was booed when he scored and booed even more when he didn't. In fact, people would go to Maple Leaf Gardens just for the pleasure of heckling Mahovlich.

Mahovlich's erratic play was so frustrating that Leafs owner, Harold Ballard, said, "Someone should give Mahovlich a punch in the nose before they drop the puck. It might make him mad and that's what he needs. A superstar has to have a mean streak in him, but Frank doesn't and that's what he lacks."

"He's as nice a man as I've ever known in this game," Toronto's assistant manager King Clancy said of Mahovlich in 1967. "Perhaps that is his trouble. He has the talent to be the greatest hockey player who ever lived if only he was a little meaner. But he isn't and there is nothing anyone can do about it."

There were nights when Mahovlich was the greatest hockey player. During a 1967 game against the Canadiens, Mahovlich picked up a rebound in his end. In that strong, sweeping glide of his, Mahovlich skated towards the Montreal zone. First he cut past Bobby Rousseau, then he muscled by J.C. Tremblay and fired a rocket that goalie Charlie Hodge stopped. Mahovlich didn't stop though. He continued around the back of the net, fought off Ted Harris, and swept the rebound into the net. The goal brought fans to their feet.

"It was a Babe Ruth home run, a Jackie Parker touchdown," wrote Jim Hunt of the *Toronto Star.* "[The play] was as close to ballet as athletics is likely to get."

With one amazing play, Frank Mahovlich could change an entire game. As one Leafs teammate said at the time, "When he's moving, he's like a man playing with boys."

In the eyes of Leafs fans, these moments were few and far between. Most of the time, Mahovlich was invisible on the ice; fans saw him as a big, lazy player who didn't pass enough, but passed too much; who didn't shoot, but shot too much.

Controversy was nothing new for Mahovlich. It had followed him since he was a 15 year old playing hockey in Timmins, Ontario. During those years, the NHL didn't have a draft. Instead, they had to send scouts across the country to find talent. Once they found a potential recruit, the scout became a salesman who had to convince the boy's parents to sign with his team. Five NHL teams, including Chicago, Detroit, Toronto, New York, and Montreal, sent scouts to entice Mahvolich's father, Peter Sr., into letting them put the boy on their negotiation list.

"I offered him everything," recalled former Chicago coach, Rudy Pilous, who was a scout at the time. "I even offered the old man a four-acre fruit farm in Niagara. A lot of good it did."

After offering Peter Sr. a deal that would see Frank join the Wings' farm team in Hamilton and attend a Catholic high school, Detroit scout Johnny Wilson left convinced he'd reached an agreement and that the two men had even shaken hands on it.

However, no one was able to top the Maple Leafs' offer. Through scout Bob Davidson, the team offered to enroll Mahovlich at St. Mike's College. Mahovlich would play for the St. Mike's hockey team, and the Leafs would pay Mahovlich's tuition, room and board, and provide him with a small weekly allowance.

The following autumn, Mahovlich enrolled at St. Mike's and starred with their Ontario Hockey Association junior team for three seasons. In his final season, the 19 year old averaged over a goal a game and finished third in scoring with 88 points. That was enough for the Leafs. Although he was eligible for a fourth season of junior play, the Leafs, who were a team in disarray at the time, felt he was ready for the jump to the NHL. The Leafs management felt that Mahovlich's explosive speed and power and his natural goal scoring ability were just what the offensively starved team needed.

The Mahovlich signing garnered heavy media attention in Toronto. Hopes were so high that Toronto's general manager, Hap Day, deemed the 19 year old "Moses" because "he can lead the Leafs out of the wilderness." *Toronto Star* columnist Red Burnett later shortened the moniker to "The Big M." Mahovlich would be the player to lead the Leafs out of the darkness to the Stanley Cup.

Mahovlich didn't let them down. He scored an impressive 15 goals and 22 points during the first half of the 1957–1958 season. However, in what became a familiar Mahovlich pattern, the winger scored only 5 goals and 14 points in the second half of the season. Despite the slump, Mahovlich still managed to edge out Chicago's Bobby Hull for the 1957–1958 Calder Trophy as best rookie. Mahovlich was not pleased with his performance and felt that Bobby Hull was more consistent and deserving of the award.

"I thought I did very badly in the second half of the season," said Mahovlich after winning the Calder Trophy. "Maybe I let up and relaxed a little too much after New Year's. I didn't intend to and I don't really know what happened. I was hoping that I could finish the season with a rush like I finished the first half. I didn't and I feel I let a lot of people down."

More importantly, the addition of Mahovlich did not lift the team out of the "wilderness"; the Leafs finished the season in last place.

Mahovlich followed his rookie season with a slightly better sophomore year in which he scored 22 goals and had 49 points. However, in season three, Mahovlich stumbled, and as he did, the critics, who would hound him throughout his Leafs tenure, came out of the shed.

"What's wrong with Mahovlich?" they asked after his disappointing 1959–1960 season.

"What makes Mahovlich tick?" asked another newspaper.

He was being booed regularly. Journalists were calling him lazy. In just one year, a year which saw the Leafs make it to the Stanley Cup finals before losing to Montreal, Mahovlich suddenly went from saviour to scapegoat. All this negative reaction was focused at a 22 year old player who had scored almost twice as many goals in his first three seasons as Gordie Howe had in his first three.

"What do they want from my life?" said Mahovlich at the time. "I score 60 goals in three seasons, and everyone still wants to know what's wrong with Mahovlich. They don't recall my good games, but they do recall my bad games. … Too many people think athletes are robots. We're not — we have our off days, just as filing clerks and insurance salesmen have their off days."

In 1960–1961, Mahovlich finally played like a superstar. Two thirds of the way through the season, he had scored 40 goals, more goals than any Leaf had scored in an entire season. With 14 games remaining, Mahovlich had 48 goals, two less than Maurice Richard's record of 50. It seemed certain that Richard's famous record would fall. Those two goals never came. Mahovlich, perhaps overwhelmed by the pressure, fell into a slump. Montreal's Bernie Geoffrion overtook him late in the year and tied the Rocket's record. Typically, rather than celebrate Mahovlich's great achievement, the Toronto media instead wondered what Mahovlich was missing that prevented him from being an even greater player.

However, if Toronto didn't appreciate Mahvolich, other teams sure did.

As the 1962–1963 season began, Mahovlich and the Leafs had been unable to agree on a contract. Mahovlich had been earning $15,000 annually, but he felt that he deserved a $10,000 raise. The Leafs countered with an insulting $1,000 raise. Mahovlich refused and left the team.

During the all-star game festivities that began the season, the Mahovlich holdout was a favourite topic. Chicago owner Jim Norris was particularly interested in the Mahovlich situation.

A night earlier, Hawks superstar, Bobby Hull, had told Norris to "get that big sucker. Toronto doesn't know how to use him. We'll put him at centre and just let him go!"

After the annual all-star game dinner in 1962, Chicago Black Hawks owner Jim Norris invited the other team owners to his room for a drink. During the course of the lively conservation, the subject of Frank Mahovlich came up. At one point, Norris said, "I'd give a million dollars to be able to negotiate with that guy. I wouldn't have any trouble signing him."

The comment surprised Maple Leaf Gardens Executive Vice-President Harold Ballard. "You what? You'd give how much to be able to sign him?"

"You heard me," said Norris. "I'd give a million dollars."

"You got a deal," said Ballard, as he winked at Leafs President Stafford Smythe.

Norris immediately took out his wallet and handed Ballard $1,000. "That's a deposit," said Norris.

Although Smythe thought it was all a joke, Ballard took the money and shook hands with Norris. Norris then told Hawks' general manager Tommy Ivan to call the wire services and tell them, "We got Mahovlich."

The next morning, Norris signed a cheque for $1 million dollars and asked Ivan to deliver it to Stafford Smythe. Meanwhile, the story had reached the press. Mahovlich's dad was stunned when he read the headlines.

He called Frank immediately and said, "You've been sold to Chicago. Apparently they bought you for a million dollars."

A bewildered Mahovlich then got a call from the Leafs asking him to head down to the Gardens immediately. When Mahovlich arrived at the Gardens, there was a horde of reporters and fans trying to get to the bottom of the story. Was it true? Was Mahovlich one of the Black Hawks? Mahovlich couldn't even give them an answer. He had no idea who he was playing for.

When Clancy and Imlach saw Mahovlich, they immediately took him into an office and presented him with a four-year contract worth $110,000. Mahovlich signed.

"I thought I won the argument," Mahovlich later said. "Well, I didn't really. I should have been getting $100,000 instead of $25,000."

Jim Norris, owner of the Black Hawks, was not pleased and unleashed a stream of bad press on the Leafs. It turned out that Ballard had no authority to approve the deal. Stafford's father, Conn, had sold his shares as Leafs owner but still had considerable influence on the team. When he learned of the deal, he immediately cancelled it.

The Leafs were embarrassed and angry. Thanks to Norris, Mahovlich had discovered his worth and beaten management at their game. From that moment on, the relationship between Mahovlich and the Leafs went very sour.

"From 1962 on," Mahovlich said later, "I had trouble with management. I never really felt comfortable with the team after 1962. It was a real drag on me."

Although Mahovlich scored 36 goals that season and the Leafs won the Stanley Cup for the second straight year, it wasn't enough for Leafs fans. Every time he stepped onto the ice, he was booed. When he was a game star, he was booed. If he scored five points in a game, he was booed. When he scored only two points in the 1963 playoffs, Mahovlich was booed during and after the Leafs' cup-clinching game. He was even heckled during the Stanley Cup victory reception the following day.

Mahovlich never let on that the booing bothered him. "I don't worry about it because I can't change things anyway," he said. "Why bother to fight other people's attitudes? They pay good money for a ticket and if they want to boo me that's their privilege."

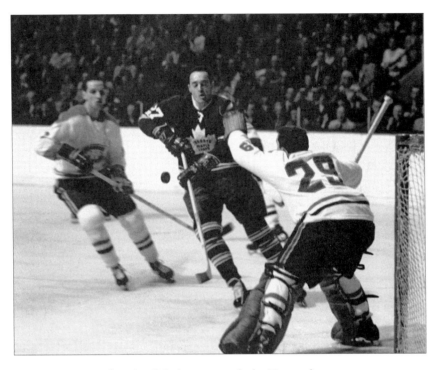

Frank Mahovlich skates towards the Montreal crease.

However, teammate Carl Brewer suggested that "it was hard on Frank and we knew it. We were glad it wasn't us, but it was hard on Frank. If you think about it, it was a credit to his greatness because the fans wouldn't accept anything less from Frank than what they perceived to be great."

Punch Imlach was another matter. Whenever Mahovlich had a good game, Imlach would intentionally mispronounce his name as "Ma-hal-o-vich" and then refer back to an earlier poor performance. On a least one occasion, Imlach insisted that Mahovlich continue to practise even though he'd given the rest of the team the afternoon off.

In general, Imlach's practices were draconian. He often sat on a chair in the middle of the rink and made the players skate for one hour. "You couldn't practise like that everyday," said Mahovlich. "If the practise was creative, I didn't mind, but it was like a punishment."

Rather than rest players and keep them energized for big games, Imlach would work them even harder at practise. Come playoff time, Mahovlich was exhausted. "If you take a horse and run the day before a race," Mahovlich said later, "he won't be the same. He'll have run the race, before the race. That's why in Toronto I had a difficult time. I left too many games on the practice ice."

Mahovlich's teammate, Carl Brewer, agreed, "The games, for me, were a chance to relax and get ready for the next week of practice because that was the only time you could have a let down."

"Every guy on the team hated Imlach," added Brewer. Although team morale was awful, Imlach managed to lead the team to four Stanley Cups in the 60s.

In November 1964, Mahovlich finally reached his breaking point and was admitted to Toronto General Hospital for severe exhaustion and depression. Of course, the Leafs did not admit that Mahovlich was suffering from depression. Rather than coming up with a good cover, the Leafs had

Mahovlich under tight security at the hospital. The secrecy drew even more attention to the matter, and soon the papers and radio were rampant with speculation. *The Globe and Mail* suspected it was mononucleosis. One radio broadcaster even thought it was cancer and that Mahovlich was going to die.

Mahovlich's spirits were buoyed by the many letters he received at the hospital from supportive Toronto fans. "There was a flood of mail for Frank, care of Maple Leaf Gardens," his wife Marie told an interviewer, "so I went down there and just took it with me. One of the cards was from Bobby Rousseau of the Montreal Canadiens."

Mahovlich remained in hospital for a month and returned to the team in December. When he stepped on the ice for the first time, the Maple Leaf Gardens fans gave him a standing ovation. Amazingly, Mahovlich still led the team in scoring that year with 51 points. However, the team missed the playoffs for the first time in four years.

The following season, Mahovlich decided he'd had enough of hockey. "I didn't want to play on that team anymore. I didn't want to go through what I went through the previous year. Around 1966, I decided I'd quit playing hockey."

During the summer, though, Mahovlich had second thoughts. In July, his wife Marie gave birth to their daughter, Nancy. The Leafs' early playoff exit that year also gave Mahovlich time to relax and rejuvenate. Meanwhile, the Leafs told Mahovlich they didn't want him to quit. By summer's end, Mahovlich's retirement plans were postponed.

By 1966–1967, the Leafs were a team in disarray. Mahovlich's goal production dropped to 18, and the team finished in third place. With the team struggling, it was Imlach's turn to suffer. In February 1967, he was forced to temporarily leave the team because of exhaustion. With King Clancy filling in as interim coach, the team flourished and put together a 10-game winning streak. Incredibly, when Imlach returned, he said that it was the hard work he'd made the team do before he left that had led to the turnaround.

Prior to the playoffs, the players rallied together and decided to win the cup just to show up Leafs management. "We'd get together and have a meeting," said Mahovlich, "and guys would be peeved off at the way management was. [Allan] Stanley would say, 'Let's win in spite of them!'" The Leafs were a team of veterans, and many of them realized that this might be their last opportunity to play for the Stanley Cup.

The Leafs surprised the Black Hawks in six games in the first round and advanced to the Stanley Cup finals against their archrival, the Montreal Canadiens. It couldn't have been scripted any better. Here were Canada's two great teams competing for the Stanley Cup during Canada's centennial year. It was also the last year of the Original Six. The following season, the NHL would add six American teams to the league. Although it wasn't a banner playoff for Mahovlich (he

Frank Mahovlich

scored only 3 goals in 12 games), it turned out to be a memorable final for the Leafs. Led by incredible performances from goalies Terry Sawchuk and Johnny Bower, the Leafs upset the heavily favoured Canadiens and won the Stanley Cup.

Mahovlich started the next season, but it wasn't long before he returned to hospital. Following a game on November 1 against the Montreal Canadiens, Mahovlich got three points and was named a star of the game. As he took his bow at the end of the game, Toronto fans greeted him with a mix of boos and cheers.

The next day, as the team was getting ready to take a train to Detroit, Mahovlich got up and went home. He immediately checked himself into the hospital. He was once again suffering from severe depression. Some reports even suggested that he'd had a nervous breakdown.

According to Mahovlich's wife, Marie, the doctor said, "Frank, there's nothing wrong with you. You have an allergy, and the allergy is Punch Imlach — and that's all that is wrong with you. ...[y]ou can't work for that man...."

At the end of November, Mahovlich returned to the lineup and played well. By the end of February 1968, rumours were rampant that Mahovlich was going to be traded to Detroit. On March 3, 1968, that's just what happened. The blockbuster trade sent Mahovlich, Pete Stemkowski, Garry Unger, and the rights to Carl Brewer to the Red Wings in exchange for Paul Henderson, Norm Ullman, and Floyd Smith.

Predictably unpredictable, Toronto fans were outraged by the trade. Maple Leaf Gardens received hundreds of calls from indignant and emotional callers the minute the trade was announced. Other fans stood outside the arena in protest. Shares in Maple Leaf Gardens even dropped. The trade brought an end to one of the most bizarre, exciting, and stormy relationships in NHL history.

Freed from the pressure and conflict in Toronto, Mahovlich experienced a rebirth in Detroit. Playing on a line with Gordie Howe and Alex Delveccio, Mahovlich had his best goal-scoring season ever, scoring 49 goals in his first full season with the team.

"When I got to Detroit," said Mahovlich, "I found their system was completely different and it suited me just fine. They played me different, their practices were different, everything was different. I never really felt I reached my potential with Toronto. Detroit just opened everything up and my output doubled. It was like a piano had been lifted off my back — I finally felt like playing."

After three successful and happy seasons in Detroit, Mahovlich was traded to the Montreal Canadiens in January 1971. The Red Wings were a struggling team and decided to dump salaries so they could rebuild. Mahovlich was disappointed to leave Detroit, but he was also excited to be joining his younger brother, Peter, with one of hockey's greatest franchises.

"Right off the bat I found things very settling in Montreal.

It was a good hockey team. We had some young players and some veterans — the mix was great."

Mahovlich was just what the Canadiens needed. He exploded during the playoffs with a record 14 goals and, along with rookie goalie Ken Dryden, led the Canadiens to a Stanley Cup championship. Mahovlich was overwhelmed after the Canadiens victory. "In Montreal you felt like cheering, you felt like having a party — it was very enjoyable." For Mahovlich, 1971 was his most satisfying year in the NHL.

In 1972, Mahovlich was invited to join Team Canada for their eight game series against the Soviet Union. Although the series has become a landmark event in Canadian history, for Mahovlich it was an experience soured by politics and greed.

"The players felt obliged to play. They didn't ask you if you wanted to play, they kind of told you. There was a lot of ill feeling because Bobby Hull didn't play. He'd just jumped ship to the [World Hockey Association]. If it was Team Canada, where was Bobby Hull? So it was really Team NHL."

Mahovlich stayed with the Canadiens until the newly formed World Hockey Association (WHA) came calling. The Toronto Toros offered Mahovlich a four-year deal worth almost twice what he was making with the Canadiens. Mahovlich accepted the offer.

"In 1974, I was 36 years old, so it was decision time. I had hardly made any money in the NHL, and the pension wasn't any good. Montreal offered me a contract, but I had this opportunity to go to the WHA. So it was a money situation."

In 18 NHL seasons, Mahovlich scored 503 goals, played in 15 all-star games, and won six Stanley Cups … not bad for a guy Toronto fans and media once called lazy.

Mahovlich remained with the Toronto Toros, later called the Birmingham Bulls, until he retired from hockey in 1978. He was elected to the Hockey Hall of Fame in 1981. In 1998, he was appointed to the Canadian Senate by Prime Minister Jean Chretien.

* * *

After scoring his 500th goal against Vancouver, Mahovlich reminded his former teammate, Jean Beliveau, of a night years earlier. "Do you remember what you said to me one night in Toronto while I was with the Leafs and we were about to face-off?"

Beliveau shook his head.

"You told me," Mahovlich continued, "I was with the wrong team. You said my style would fit in best with the Canadiens' style."

"I was right," said Beliveau.

Mahovlich simply smiled. He was satisfied, finally.

Chapter 7
Bobby Hull

ith a powerful line-up that included Bobby Hull and other future NHLers like Stan Mikita, Johnny McKenzie, and Chico Maki, the St. Catharine's Teepees of the Ontario Hockey Association were expected to contend for the Memorial Cup during the 1957–1958 season. Those hopes died in September 1957. The Black Hawks regularly held their training camp in St. Catharines. The New York Rangers were in town for an exhibition game against the Hawks. Hull had spent the morning working out at the rink. In the afternoon, he played a high school football game. In the middle of dinner, Hull received a phone call from a Black Hawks scout asking him to come to the rink. He wolfed down his dinner, hurried to the rink — and scored two goals against the Rangers.

"That night," said Hull, "the Hawks signed me to a major-league contract." Hull became one of the youngest players ever to join the NHL. The timing was perfect.

The NHL's image was souring in the USA. With the exception of the Detroit Red Wings, the American teams were routinely finishing in the bottom half of the league standings. Aside from Gordie Howe, none of these teams had any marketable stars to capture the imaginations of the American hockey fan. The Montreal Canadiens were loaded with talent, but none of their stars were well-known outside of Canada. While television had taken hockey to a wider audience in Canada, US networks largely ignored the sport.

"The NHL badly needed a star with oomph and appeal," said former Black Hawks coach Rudy Pilous, "to get some attention in the US."

With a marketable star, the NHL might have an opportunity to attract new American fans and perhaps even earn some television revenue. Bobby Hull was just what the sport needed. He was made for TV. Everything about Hull was visually exciting.

"Hull arrived with his speed and flair and good looks, the blond hair, the big slapshot, the total package who gave off the feeling that he was a bit of a rascal. There was a void and he filled it full," remarked Pilous.

"The sight of Robert Marvin Hull ... " wrote *Time Magazine* in 1968, "leaning into a hockey puck is one of the true spectacles of sport — like watching Mickey Mantle clear the roof, or Wilt Chamberlain flick in a basket, or Bart Starr throw that beautiful bomb."

Fans, in particular, adored Hull's outgoing personality. His willingness to sign autographs for hours was legendary. As an issue of *The Sport Special* read: "Teammates talk with awe of seeing Hull, at one in the morning in an airport, sit down at a table and sign autographs for a hundred people. … Newspapermen in NHL cities talk of his good-humoured willingness to answer questions gracefully in victory or in defeat."

Hull's appeal went beyond hockey. Middle-aged women sighed and young girls who couldn't care less about hockey had his poster up on the walls of their rooms. *Chicago Daily News* society page columnist, Tish Baldridge, described Hull as "a man who inspires sighs in every maiden and envy in the blood of every man."

"Hull was youthful and photogenic and he almost percolated with testosterone," wrote Rosie DiManno in the book, *Remembering the Golden Jet.* "Those muscled biceps, those huge hands, that trademark smile, verging on leer. … Here, unexpectedly, was hockey's first sex symbol."

While stars like Gordie Howe and Frank Mahovlich often seemed uncomfortable in the spotlight, Hull thrived on the attention. Win or lose, Hull was always accessible to the media and fans. "Inscribed indelibly into the folklore of hockey," wrote reporter Earl McRae in 1971, "is the scene that shows a dark and empty parking lot in winter, long after the game has ended, with the solitary figure of Bobby Hull standing surrounded by dozens of children thrusting pieces of paper at him, calling for his attention. Hull, the superstar, stands there until he signs every last scrap."

"If people think enough of me to want to shake my hand, talk to me, or interview me," Hull said during the peak of his popularity, "then time must be made for it."

Bobby Hull was only 14 when the Chicago Black Hawks first expressed interest in him. He was playing in a Bantam league in Belleville, Ontario, when Hawks' scout Bob Wilson noticed the boy's unusual speed and power. Wilson watched Hull play a few more games and then urged the Hawks to sign the boy to their negotiation list. They agreed and sent Wilson to sign the boy. Wilson met with Hull's father, Robert, and told him that the Hawks wanted to move the boy to their Junior B team in Hespeler. The Hawks would cover his tuition and expenses. Hull's father agreed, and Bobby's hockey career was under way. Soon after, Hull was transferred to the Hawks' team in Woodstock before being promoted to the St. Catharine's Teepees. He stayed with the Teepees for two years before his surprise promotion to the big leagues.

Hull's first season was decent, but not great. He didn't score his first goal until the seventh game of the season and scored only 13 all season. The following year, coach Rudy Pilous moved Hull from centre to left wing. The move eventually paid off. In his third season, Hull exploded for 39 goals and 42 assists to win the Art Ross Trophy as the NHL's leading scorer. Hull solidified his superstar status the following season when he helped lead the Black Hawks to their first Stanley Cup in 12 years. The legend of the Golden Jet, so nicknamed because of his speed and blonde hair, was born. Hull was now approaching the status of Joe Namath and Mickey Mantle as a universally recognized sports star.

It was in his fifth season that the Golden Jet's mystique really took flight. Up to that point, Hull's game was a combination of power and speed. He had powerful legs and a strong upper body, and he was capable of hitting top speed in a flash. He also possessed the most feared weapon in the history of hockey — the slapshot. One of the game's most memorable images was Hull roaring down the wing into the opposing zone, then doing a quick shuffle to create space, and winding up to deliver his cannonball of a shot.

Prior to the 1961–1962 season, Hull added a new dimension to his slapshot: the curved blade. He had gotten the idea from teammate Stan Mikita. The curved blade gave the player the feeling that he was catching the puck and then flinging it — almost like a lacrosse player — at the goal.

"You can pull the puck into you and shoot it at the same time," Hull once recalled. "If you tried the same thing with a straight blade, you'd just pull the puck into the corner."

Not only did goalies have to contend with Hull's power, they had to figure out where the shot was going.

"I always thought that the curve made the puck spin

when I hit it right, then dip, like an old drop-ball in baseball, before it got to the net," said Hull.

As journalist Frank Orr once wrote: "The puck came off the curved blade of a hockey stick that started straight up in the air like a golfer on the tee, except that the "tee" and the swinger were moving at 30 miles per hour, the 'hook' in the blade causing the puck to dip, curve, and flutter on its way to the net."

With or without a curve, goalies throughout the league spoke with a mixture of fear and amazement of Hull's shot, which was once clocked by hockey fitness expert Lloyd Percival at 119.5 miles per hour.

"His shot is like a piece of lead," said Rangers' goalie, Jacques Plante, at the time. "One of his hard shots would break my mask. I've caught one on the arm and it was paralysed for five minutes afterwards. Sometimes it drops four or five inches. You have to see it to believe it."

Gump Worsley was once hit in the face by a Hull shot, but he considered himself fortunate because "the flat side of the puck hit me. If it had been the edge of the puck, well, they could have called the undertaker."

Ken Dryden of the Montreal Canadiens was so mystified by Hull's power that he used math to calculate the impossibility of stopping a 120 miles per hour Hull shot from 60 feet out. "At that speed, the puck goes from the stick to the net in 0.352 seconds. In that minute bit of time, my brain can't decide what to do, tell my hand to lift, and have my hand obey the command."

Chicago's legendary goalie, Glenn Hall, hated his team-mate's shot so much that he often reported to training camp late.

"He always said he was painting the barn," said former Black Hawks coach Rudy Pilous. "He just didn't like facing Hull's slapshot every goddamn day."

During practices, Hall would sometimes leave the net when Hull approached to fire one of his missiles. "There are days," said Hall, "when you just step aside and leave the door wide open. It's a simple act of self-preservation."

When Hull's turn came to shoot, he'd fire the puck into the corner at Hall.

Hall wasn't the only person in danger. "During practice," Hall recalled in the biography, *The Man They Call Mr. Goalie,* "the cleaning ladies would be working in the stands and when one would bend over, Bobby would shoot a puck at a seat next to where they'd be working. It got to the point where they refused to work while we were practising."

To appease everyone and ease his goalie's anxiety, coach Pilous often used a wooden dummy in the net during practices. Hull didn't care. He just kept launching his rockets.

It was no coincidence that Hull's new "banana blade," as it was nicknamed, helped him threaten Maurice Richard's remarkable scoring record of 50 goals in 50 games. In later years, so many players reached the 50-goal plateau that it lost a bit of its mystique. However, in the 1960s, the 50-goal mark was a pinnacle of individual achievement in hockey.

At the time, Maurice Richard's 1944–1945 record was akin to Babe Ruth's 60 home runs in baseball, which was held for 35 years until Roger Maris broke it. It was a barrier that seemed impossible to topple.

Even with the NHL's longer schedule of 70 games, no player had managed to topple Richard's record. The great Gordie Howe mustered only 49 goals. In the 1960–1961 season, Bernie "Boom Boom" Geoffrion and Frank Mahovlich came close. Geoffrion stalled at 50, and the record seemed sure to fall when Frank Mahovlich had 43 goals after 55 games. Unfortunately, Mahovlich went into a slump and only managed five goals in the remaining 14 games to finish with 48.

It was felt that if anyone could break the record, it was Bobby Hull. Even Rocket Richard admitted, "Bobby Hull could be the first player to score 60 goals in a single season."

Hull came close in 1961–1962 when he hit goal number 50 in the final game of the season. It was later discovered that Hull had unofficially scored 51 goals that season, but a mid-season goal against Detroit was mistakenly credited to Hull's teammate, Ab McDonald.

The NHL had taken notice, and opposing teams went out of their way to put the Golden Jet off his game.

During the next three seasons, Hull could only muster 31, 43, and 39 goals. In the 1964–1965 season, Hull scored 35 goals in his first 37 games and seemed a sure bet to break Richard's record. However, a stream of opposing obstructions and injuries slowed him down, and he finished with 39 goals in 61 games.

Tommy Ivan of the Black Hawks complained that referees were ignoring the flagrant abuses being given to Hull. "It's not that Bobby isn't playing well enough to score 51 or 61 goals; he's just not being allowed to play his game. He's hooked and held and tripped more than any man in the league."

His opponents agreed. "He'll beat you unless you stay right on top of him, and it's harder than ever to do that," said Boston forward, Leo Boivin. "You have to try and get him over to the boards. It isn't easy. He's like a bull."

Once Hull found his speed, he was almost unstoppable, so the approach was to check, hook, and generally harass him before he could move into fast gear. Given the intense on-ice harassment, Hull's patience was almost superhuman. Following the season, he won the league's Lady Byng Trophy for gentlemanly play. Even with the constant hooking, holding, and checking by his opponents, he had only 32 minutes in penalties.

After failing to top Richard's record of hitting 50 goals in 1961–1962, Chicago fans were beginning to wonder if Hull would ever be able to do it. In the 1965–1966 season, Hull finally delivered. Despite enduring nagging knee and hand injuries that forced him to miss five games, and not scoring in 30 of the 65 games he did play in, Hull scored in streaks, and he had scored goal 50 by the season's 57th game.

Bobby Hull

From there, the excitement grew. The media followed Hull daily, and the atmosphere prior to a Saturday night game on March 5, 1966 at Maple Leaf Gardens was jumping with anticipation. There were feature stories in major newspapers and on national television. If the pressure was getting to Hull, he didn't show it. However, the Black Hawks team certainly seemed to show it. Chicago lost 5–0 to Toronto, and in the next two games, they were shut out by Montreal and then New York. A Chicago paper even asked "Will Hawks Ever Score Again?"

The drought continued in the next game as the Hawks found themselves down 2–0 to the Rangers to start the third period. Chico Maki finally ended the drought early in the third to make the score 2–1. Six minutes into the period, the Black Hawks went on the power play. Hull picked up the puck near the Hawks' blue line and skated towards the Rangers' zone. As linemate Eric Nesterenko drove to the net, Hull wound up and fired a shot past Rangers' goalie, Cesare Maniago. The shot was so hard that Hull nearly fell over.

"I moved the puck out front for a slapshot," Hull said later. "I got it out too far and almost topped it, didn't get real good wood on the thing, and it skidded away, skimming on the ice."

"I saw the puck all the way," said Maniago. "I intended to play the damn thing with my stick, and just at the crucial second, Nesterenko cut across from my left and lifted my stick. He gave me no chance to make a play."

The capacity crowd in Chicago went crazy. One paper compared it to Times Square on VE day, the day World War II ended. "Hats — enough to stock a store — an umbrella, a model of a golden jet plane, disks bearing number 51, coins, and just plain garbage rained down on the ice as the red light glowed behind the New York goal."

The game was paused, and Hull skated around the ice chased by photographers. Through the rink side glass, Hull's wife kissed his hand and smiled. Later, Hull picked up a high silk hat, placed it on his head, and waved to the crowd. After almost 10 minutes, the applause finally petered out and the game resumed.

Hull finished the season with a record 54 goals. He also beat Dickie Moore's scoring record by one point, finishing with 97 points. From that moment on, there was no stopping the Golden Jet.

After setting the record, endorsements poured in for Hull. He endorsed swimsuits, sweaters, and hair tonics. He appeared in magazine and TV advertisements. He recorded a radio show, became an advisor to Simpsons-Sears department store, and endorsed his own line of hockey gear. There was even a Bobby Hull table hockey game. Bobby Hull Enterprises became involved with the manufacturing of air conditioners, vinyl car mats, and cardboard boxes. By 1965, half of Hull's $60,000 per year income was coming from endorsements.

"I've seen too many players," said Hull in defence of his outside income, "go through this league and after 10 years they're out and the big money stops coming in. I feel I owe it to my family and my future to cash in what I can."

Some worried that Hull was more concerned with making money than playing hockey. In 1968, he missed the Hawks training camp to get a $100,000 business deal. When he returned, Hull responded by beating his goal and point scoring record with 58 goals and 107 points.

By 1970, the relationship between the Black Hawks and Hull was souring. While Hull soared individually, the Black Hawks continually fell short. Part of the problem was the team played a freewheeling style that relied too heavily on Hull and Stan Mikita. Without a dependable goalie (Glenn Hall was signed by St. Louis in the 1967 expansion draft) and a solid defence, this wide-open system failed and the team gave up as many goals as they scored. The team worked to fix the problem, when in 1969, they landed goalie Tony Esposito in a trade with Montreal. Meanwhile, coach Billy Reay installed a defensive system to cut down on Hull's improvised attacks and force the team to take a more disciplined approach. Hull scored only 38 goals that season.

Off the ice, Hull began to have contract problems with the Black Hawks. He held out in 1968 and 1970 to get more money from the Hawks. The situation finally reached a boiling point in 1972.

The World Hockey Association (WHA), a new professional hockey league, was ready to start their inaugural season. The WHA knew that if they had any hope of surviving, they needed a recognizable hockey star. The league knew of Hull's money problems with the Black Hawks. The owner of their new franchise, the Winnipeg Jets, approached Hull as soon as his NHL contract expired after the 1971–1972 season. Initially, Hull was using the Jets to lure a richer contract from the Black Hawks, but the Hawks wouldn't offer more than $100,000 per season. When the WHA agreed to give Hull an astounding $1 million dollar signing bonus along with a salary of $250,000 per year, Hull's days as an NHL player were pretty much done. The Hawks quickly countered with an offer of $200,000 per season, but it was too late. Hull accepted the Jets' offer. The NHL had just lost its biggest and brightest star. The face of professional hockey was forever changed.

Hull's signing had a monumental impact on professional hockey. Not only did his signing give the WHA life, but in doing so, it opened the floodgates on player salaries. After decades of being forced to submit to the low-ball contract offers from NHL teams, the players had some options, thanks to the WHA and Bobby Hull.

The NHL didn't back down. First, NHL president, Clarence Campbell, approached the US Senate with the claim that Hull was the property of the Black Hawks. Then the Hawks went to court to try and prevent Hull from playing in the WHA. By the time all the legal tape was untangled and a judge finally ruled that Hull was not the property of the Black Hawks or the NHL, Hull had missed the Jets' first 14 games.

However, the NHL wasn't finished with Hull just yet. The league caused a national crisis when it declared that Hull would banned from playing for Team Canada, who were already without the injured Bobby Orr, in the upcoming Summit Series that pitted Canada's best hockey players against the stars of the Soviet Union. Hockey fans, reporters, and even Canadian politicians were outraged. Former Prime Minister John Diefenbaker called the decision "petty," while Prime Minister Pierre Trudeau sent telegrams to leading hockey officials encouraging them that it was in the best interests of Canada to include Hull on the team. He later told reporters that he hoped those behind the decision would see the light and "be big enough to respond to the clear desire of Canadians" to let Hull play.

"I don't give a damn if Hull signed with a team in China," declared an outraged Maple Leafs owner, Harold Ballard. "He's Canadian and should be on Team Canada."

The NHL refused to budge.

"That was the only disappointment of my career," Hull said in 2003. "It hurt because I was a Canadian and I've always been a Canadian. And all of a sudden, just because I opted to go to another team in Canada from Chicago, I'm not Canadian enough to play for them."

Hull eventually got to play the Soviets in two tournaments. In 1974, the WHA formed its own version of Team Canada. Canada lost the eight game series, but Hull was one of the standouts of the series. Hull finally got to play with Canada's best team in 1976 when Hockey Canada created the Canada Cup tournament, later called the World Cup. By this time, the rules were changed to allow participating countries to use players from any league. Led by Hull, Bobby Orr and Rogie Vachon, Canada won the inaugural tournament.

Meanwhile, Hull continued his high scoring ways in the WHA. In seven seasons with the Winnipeg Jets, Hull scored 303 goals and led the team to three Avco Cup championships. Hull's high point came in 1974–1975 when he re-established a goal scoring record by scoring 77 goals and beating Phil Esposito's 1970–1971 record of 76.

In the end, even Bobby Hull couldn't save the WHA. A year after Hull announced his retirement in 1978, the WHA collapsed. Four of their teams — the Winnipeg Jets, Quebec Nordiques, New England Whalers, and the Edmonton Oilers (along with a youngster named Wayne Gretzky) — moved to the NHL.

Hull returned briefly to the NHL in 1979–1980. He played 18 games with the Jets before joining the Hartford (formerly New England) Whalers. Hull finished his career with the Whalers, playing nine games alongside fellow hockey immortal, Gordie Howe.

Hull's life wasn't all golden. In 1980, Hull's divorce from his wife, Joanne, made the headlines. Hull was always protective of his private life, but he couldn't stop the flood of details about mental and physical abuse. Joanne told stories of abuse that dated back to the mid-1960s. She said that in 1966 Hull had held her over a balcony after he'd hit her in the head with a shoe. After more cases of abuse, she had filed for divorce in 1970. Eventually, she reconsidered, but the final blow came in 1978 when Hull threatened her with a loaded shotgun.

In 1984, Hull remarried. Two years later, he was charged with assault and battery. The charges were later dropped, although Hull did plead guilty to taking a punch at one of the arresting police officers.

In 1998, Hull's reputation took another shot when he was quoted by the *Moscow Times* as saying that the black population in America was growing too fast and that "Hitler had some good ideas. He just went a bit too far." When asked if it would be fair to label him a racist, Hull said, "I don't give a damn. I'm not running for any political office." Hull vehemently denied making the comments.

It's easy to wipe away Hull's hockey achievements in the face of such personal infamy. Should fans even care what Bobby Hull did in his private life? Of course they should, but without the unrealistic demands and images that are all too often placed on public figures, especially athletes. Hull, like Busher Jackson, and Frank Mahovlich before him, is little more than a human. He's done good and bad, just like every one.

Having said that, one still has to question whether Bobby Hull really received the credit he deserves for his role in radically transforming the business and game of hockey. He was among the first players to use hockey to earn lucrative endorsement deals. No other player had the same impact until Wayne Gretzky joined the Los Angeles Kings.

Furthermore, Hull's decision to sign with the Winnipeg Jets opened the market up for player salaries. After years of enduring an unspoken salary cap from NHL owners, players had options. Today's millionaire players and billionaire owners owe a great deal to Bobby Hull, whom Chicago Black Hawks owner Bill Wirtz called "the best public relations man the NHL ever had."

Epilogue

Debate will always arise when compiling a collection of this sort. These extraordinary players were by no means the only great left wingers of their era. Strong cases could also be made for the inclusion of Woody Dumart of the Boston Bruins, Montreal's Toe Blake, Sweeney Schriner of the New York Americans, Babe Siebert of the Montreal Maroons, the Red Wings' Sid Abel, Cy Denneny of the Ottawa Senators, and Bun Cook of the Rangers — all of whom are deserving members of the Hockey Hall of Fame.

With the exception of Frank Mahovlich and Bobby Hull, this book could easily be a celebration of hockey's many unsung heroes. As talented and successful as Joliat, Bentley, Moore, Lindsay, and Jackson were on their own, their exploits were often overshadowed by superstar linemates like Howie Morenz, Charlie Conacher, Gordie Howe, Max Bentley or, in Dickie Moore's case, most of the Montreal Canadiens roster. An additional difficulty for Aurel Joliat, Doug Bentley, Dickie Moore, and Ted Lindsay was size. They were all smaller and more fragile than the average NHL player.

In the face of such obstacles, these players had to work harder and think faster than their more naturally gifted colleagues. What made this group so special and successful was that they wanted to do more than survive. They wanted to be the best. It wasn't enough to take a pounding; they had to give it back twice as good. It wasn't enough to be fast; they had to be faster. In the end, each of these players proved that they belonged and that they were just as good without their superstar colleagues by their side. More than talent and size, it was their heart and determination that made these players great left wingers and outstanding hockey players.

Bibliography

Andrahtas, Tom. *Glenn Hall: The Man they Call Mr. Goalie.* Greystone Books. 2002.

Batten, Jack. *The Leafs: An Anecdotal History of the Toronto Maple Leafs.* Key Porter Books. 1994.

Beardsley, Doug (editor). *Our Game: An All-Star Collection of Hockey Fiction.* Polestar. 1997.

Brown, Bill. *The Montreal Maroons: The Forgotten Stanley Cup Champions.* Vehicule Press. 1999

Diamond, Dan, et al. *Total Hockey: The Official Encyclopedia of the National Hockey League.* Total Sports Publishing. 2000.

Fischler, Stan. *Hockey's 100: A Personal Ranking of the Best Players in Hockey History.* Stoddart. 1984.

Fischler, Stan. *Those Were the Days: The Lore of Hockey by the Legends of the Game.* Dodd, Mead and Company. 1976.

Goyens, Chrys, and Allan Turowetz. *Lions in Winter.* Prentice-Hall. 1986.

Hewitt, Foster. *Hockey Night in Canada: The Maple Leafs' Story.* Ryerson Press. 1961.

Houston, William. *Inside Maple Leaf Gardens: The Rise and Fall of the Toronto Maple Leafs.* McGraw-Hill. 1989.

Hunter, Douglas. *Scotty Bowman: A Life in Hockey.* Triumph Books. 1999.

MacInnis, Craig (editor). *Remembering the Golden Jet: A Celebration of Bobby Hull.* Stoddart. 2001.

MacSkimming, Roy. *Gordie: A Hockey Legend.* Greystone Books. 1995.

Mahovlich, Ted. *The Big M: The Frank Mahovlich Story.* Harper-Collins. 2000.

McDonnell, Chris. *The Game I'll Never Forget: 100 Hockey Stars' Stories.* Firefly Books. 2002.

Obodiac, Stan (editor). *The Leafs: The First 50 Years.* McClelland and Stewart. 1976.

O'Brien, Andy. *Superstars: Hockey's Greatest Players.* McGraw-Hill Ryerson. 1973.

Orr, Frank. *Tough Guys of Pro Hockey.* Random House. 1974.

Selke, Frank J. *Behind the Cheering.* McClelland and Stewart. 1964.

Smythe, Conn. *If You Can't Beat 'Em in the Alley.* McClelland and Stewart. 1981.

Acknowledgments

Thanks to Jim Barber, Linda Aspen-Baxter, Kara Turner, and the fine folks at Altitude Publishing; Craig Campbell and Tyler Wolosewich at the Hockey Hall of Fame; and, as always, special thanks and love to Kelly, Betty, and Jarvis Neall.

I would also like to thank and acknowledge the many journalists and writers at *The Globe and Mail, Toronto Star, Ottawa Citizen, Montreal Gazette, The Hockey News,* the Hockey Hall of Fame "Legends" website, and various hockey publications for much of the information and the quotes contained in this book. I am particularly indebted to the writings of Stan Fischler, Don MacEachern, and Jack Batten for the material on Doug Bentley.

Photo Credits

Cover: London Life-Portnoy/Hockey Hall of Fame; Hockey Hall of Fame: pages 54, 118; Frank Prazak/Hockey Hall of Fame: pages 69, 101; James Rice/Hockey Hall of Fame: page 22.

About the Author

Chris Robinson is an author, freelance writer, and the Artistic Director of the Ottawa International Animation Festival. He also writes the "gonzo" column called "The Animation Pimp" for *Animation World Magazine*. His writing has appeared in *Take One, Cinemascope, Montage, Salon.com, Stop Smiling, The Ottawa Xpress,* and many international publications.

His books include *Between Genius and Utter Illiteracy: A Story of Estonian Animation, Ottawa Senators: Great Stories from the NHL's First Dynasty, Unsung Heroes of Animation,* and *Stole This From a Hockey Card: A Philosophy of Hockey, Doug Harvey, Identity and Booze.*

An anthology of Robinson's Animation Pimp columns will be published in 2006.

He is currently working on a novel about angels, devils, and everything in-between.

Robinson lives in Ottawa with his wife, Kelly, and son, Jarvis.

Amazing Author Question and Answer

What was your inspiration for writing about this topic?

I wanted to write about left wingers because I've always been curious about Busher Jackson and Ted Lindsay. I had already done research on both of them years before, and I had even spoken with Lindsay a few times. I found their lives inspiring, for different reasons.

What surprised you most while you were researching the topic?

I was most surprised at how influential Bobby Hull was on the game of hockey. I knew he was a great player, and I remember him playing in the WHA when I was a kid. However, I had no sense of the impact he had on bringing the NHL to a wider market. He was the Gretzky of his time.

What do you most admire about the person or people in this Amazing Story?

I admire Ted Lindsay because on and off the ice, he was/is a courageous man, truly a hero. Dickie Moore's on-ice courage was also quite amazing.

What escapade do you most identify with?

I identify most with Busher Jackson's struggle to find an identity without hockey. There's just something so human about his story.

What difficulties did you run into when researching this topic?

The most difficult guy to write about was Doug Bentley. There really hasn't been much written about him. This surprised me, considering the massive amounts of material about most of the other wingers.

What part of the writing process did you enjoy most?

Having the chance to write about Busher Jackson was the most enjoyable. I'd love to write a book about his up and down life.

Why did you become a writer? Who inspired you?

I had no choice. Writing became me. Nick Tosches was my big inspiration.

What is your next project?

It's a novel tentatively called *To A Place Worse Than This*. I'm still toiling away on a book called *Hockey on The Rocks: A History of Hockey and Alcohol*.

Who are your Canadian heroes?

Tommy Douglas is my Canadian hero.

Which other Amazing Stories would you recommend?

I would have to recommend *Ottawa Senators*, of course.

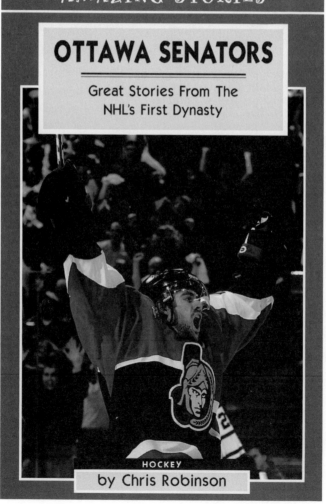

AMAZING STORIES™

OTTAWA SENATORS

Great Stories From The
NHL's First Dynasty

HOCKEY

by Chris Robinson

OTTAWA SENATORS
Great Stories From The
NHL's First Dynasty

"Ottawa tied the game on a bizarre play. Harry Smith went down after taking a vicious cross-check. Smith then slid, with the puck underneath him, into the Wanderers net. The goal counted."

The Ottawa Senators have had a long and storied history as one of the original — and dominant — Canadian franchises. Stocked with skilled and adventurous players, the early Senators were known for their aggressive play and never-say-die attitude. The fascinating story of the team continues into the present with the thrilling account of how a new franchise was secured, complete with hopes for Stanley Cups in the future.

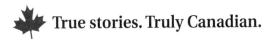 True stories. Truly Canadian.

ISBN 1-55153-790-7

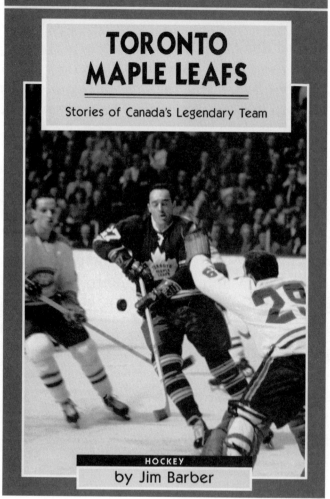

AMAZING STORIES™

TORONTO MAPLE LEAFS

Stories of Canada's Legendary Team

HOCKEY

by Jim Barber

TORONTO MAPLE LEAFS
Stories of Canada's Legendary Team

*"Since its construction in 1931, the Maple
Leaf Gardens had seen its share of powerful,
memorable moments and held its share of
championship glory. But there was something
different about this evening of May 2, 1967."*

The Toronto Maple Leafs is one of Canada's
greatest hockey franchises. From their humble
beginnings in the 1920s, to their remarkable
Stanley Cup victories of the 1940s and 1960s, to
their team-building challenges of the 1990s and
beyond, the Leafs have a history packed with
exhilarating accomplishments and devastating
setbacks. This is their story — the incredible story
of a beloved Canadian institution.

 True stories. Truly Canadian.

ISBN 1-55153-788-5

AMAZING STORIES™

GREAT STANLEY CUP VICTORIES

Glorious Moments in Hockey

HOCKEY

by Rich Mole